SEEKING

NEW YORK

SEEKING NEW YORK

THE STORIES BEHIND THE HISTORIC ARCHITECTURE
OF MANHATTAN—ONE BUILDING AT A TIME

TOM MILLER

CONTENTS

First published in the United States of America in 2015 by
Rizzoli International Publications, Inc.
300 Park Avenue South
New York, NY 10010
www.rizzoliusa.com

Originally published in the United Kingdom in 2015 as
Seeking New York
Copyright © Pimpernel Press Limited 2015
Text copyright © Tom Miller 2015
Illustrations copyright © Jenny Seddon 2015
Photographs copyright © see page 256

First Pimpernel Press edition 2015
www.pimpernelpress.com

Designed by Becky Clarke

2015 2016 2017 2018 / 10 9 8 7 6 5 4 3 2 1

ISBN: 978-0-7893-2917-2

Library of Congress Control Number: 2014950928

Printed in China

LOWER MANHATTAN

CAPTAIN JOSEPH ROSE HOUSE
273 WATER STREET

NEW YORK EVENING POST BUILDING
20 VESEY STREET

279 WATER STREET.

CAPTAIN JOSEPH ROSE HOUSE: THE RAT PIT

273 WATER STREET

When Captain Joseph Rose built his red-brick Georgian home at 273 Water Street in or around 1773, long before landfill widened Manhattan Island, the river ran just behind the property. Here Rose and his neighbor, William Laight, shared a pier where they docked their brigs. Rose's ship, the *Industry*, brought expensive mahogany from Honduras for his import trade.

Similar merchant-class homes lined the streets of the neighborhood on Water between Dover Street and Peck Slip. Rose's fashionable, wide home with the dormered attic spoke of his success.

In 1791, Rose and his family moved to Pearl Street, leaving the Water Street property to his son. Shortly after the beginning of the nineteenth century the street level of the Water Street house was converted to commercial use: first as a cobbler shop, then an apothecary. In the years before the Civil War the upper floors became a boardinghouse. By now the neighborhood had substantially declined, and Water Street had earned a reputation, in the words of James D. McCabe, writing in 1882, as a "sea of wretchedness and sin."

The author said of Water Street: "Strains of music float out into the night air, and about the doors and along the sidewalks stand groups of hideous women, waiting to entice sailors into these hells, where they are made drunk with drugged liquors, robbed of their money and valuables, and turned helpless into the streets. Groups of drunken and foul-mouthed men and boys lounge about the street, bandying vile jests with the women, and often insulting respectable passers-by."

In 1863, Christopher Burns, also known as Christopher Keyburn, purchased 273 Water Street, commencing a chapter of the building's existence that reads like a scene from Charles Dickens. The 33-year-old Burns, usually called "Kit," was one of the founders of the Dead Rabbits gang. He opened a dance hall in the house called "Sportsmen's Hall" where he offered a variety of distractions—gambling, bare-knuckle boxing, dancing, and drinking; but most notoriously, rat-versus-dog fights.

Burns kept a stable of terriers caged in the basement. Large burlap bags of brown wharf rats were brought in and released into an 8-foot-square rat pit constructed in the center of the tavern. The pit was lined in zinc, and surrounding it tiered benches provided the patrons a good view of the show. Bets were made on how quickly a dog could kill 100 rats (the record was less than 12 minutes). Patrons paid from $1.50 to $5.00 admission—about what a skilled laborer earned in a day.

Edward Winslow Martin wrote of Sportsmen's Hall in his 1868 *Secrets of the Great City*: "It is simply sickening. Most of our readers have witnessed a dog fight in the streets. Let them imagine the animals surrounded by a crowd of brutal wretches whose conduct stamps them as beneath the struggling beasts and they will have a fair idea of the scene at Kit Burns."

No hint of the house's sordid history remains in the altered and restored façade.

James McCabe added, "Some of the men will catch up the dog in their arms, and press it to their bosom in a frenzy of joy, or kiss it as if it were a human being, unmindful or careless of the fact that all this while the animal is smeared with the blood of its victims. The scene is disgusting beyond description." Making the evening even more macabre was Burns's son-in-law, Jack the Rat. Between rounds he would jump into the pit and for a dime would bite the head off a live mouse. For a quarter he would do the same with a rat.

In the late 1860s local Christian reform ministers targeted Water Street as a high-profile arena for their good works. They would take over barrooms in the afternoons for prayer meetings. Sportsmen's Hall was among those, and because of that the preachers loudly proclaimed that they had converted Kit Burns. In actuality, Burns was charging them $150 a month for the space for one hour a day from noon to 1:00 p.m.

The *Police Gazette* illustrated the sport in 1891, including the catching of rats and the dogs used.

In 1870, after an intense campaign waged by reformist Henry Bergh (who would later found the ASPCA), Sportsmen's Hall was closed down. Kit Burns, in an ironic twist, leased the building to the Williamsburg Methodist Church as a home for fallen women. He immediately opened a new rat pit at 388 Water Street.

On February 7 the church's building was dedicated. The *Times* reported, "The haunt at No. 273 Water Street, known as 'Kit Burns' Rat Pit' which has been hired by Rev. Wm. H. Boole . . . for a mission and a home for the reform of abandoned women, was yesterday dedicated . . .. A great many of the denizens of that region gathered about the entrance and Kit and his companions . . . freely expressed their disgust for the whole proceedings."

Before the year was out, Kit Burns died, not yet 40 years old.

In 1904 a fire damaged the structure, after which it was used as a warehouse. Then in 1976 another fire gutted the building. Two years later the city seized it for back taxes and it sat abandoned, an empty shell, for two decades.

Developer Frank J. Sciame, Jr., of Sciame Development Company, purchased the house in 1997 for a total cost of $1.00. Working with architect Oliver Lundquist, Sciame put $1.1 million into the renovation of the old building—now the third oldest surviving structure in Manhattan.

Completed in 1998, the renovated house has four luxury apartments. Today, in the house where Jack the Rat bit off the heads of live rodents, apartments are selling for just over $1 million.

279 WATER STREET

Comfortable brick homes lined Water Street in the last years of the eighteenth century. Ship captains and importers built their residences here, conveniently near their private piers and commercial wharfs. In 1794, Newell Narine (sometimes spelled Narme) leased from James Kip a wood-frame Georgian-style building at 279 Water Street on the corner of Dover Street. The two-and-a-half-story building housed his "grocery and wine and porter bottler" business on the ground floor while he most likely lived above.

Before landfill would later move the riverfront two blocks away, the East River's bank was just half a block to the east, where stood Lawrence's Wharf.

Two years later Narine was sent to debtor's prison, after which Kip leased the property to retired ship captain Peter Laing, who continued running the grocery with his wife, Janet. Later Laing purchased the building in what would be the first of a great many title changes. Things apparently went smoothly for two decades, then the Laings sold the business in 1826 to attorney Charles G. Ferris.

Ferris leased the building, and after his death, it was managed by his estate. As the Civil War approached, the climate of Water Street changed. Once-elegant captains' homes were converted to brothels, gambling houses, and saloons.

The proprietors of 279 Water changed rapidly. In 1847, Henry Williams opened his porter house, selling malt liquor here. In 1858, John Henry Stelling and William Brosnan ran their saloon for one year before Thomas Norton took over the lease.

The neighborhood continued to decline. In 1862, Catherine Curran was lured into the bar and murdered. According to the press, the 28-year-old Curran had been "living a dissolute course of life with a man named James Winthrop." When Winthrop left her for another woman, Honora Morrissey, the jealous Catherine stalked him for several weeks, begging that he come back to her.

After about a week, Winthrop decided that the only way to free himself of Catherine Curran was by murder. The *New York Times* reported that he " . . . in company with Honora, formed the diabolical plan of destroying her life by making her drink a mixture, composed of equal parts of burning fluid and alcohol; and incredible as it appears, witnesses testified upon the inquest that the deceased was compelled to drink three decanters full of this fiery fluid, each decanter containing a quart, in one hour. The result was death in a short time thereafter."

A less lethal crime was committed five years later, in 1867, when Samuel Norton was arrested. His bail was set at $300 for having "disposed of strong and spirituous liquors, wines, ales and beer on Sundays."

The depravity of the area prompted reformers like Jerry Macauley to attempt to introduce religion to the locals. From his Water Street Mission, Macauley railed against the saloons and brothels. On March 30, 1878, he was responsible for a raid that included 279 Water Street. Nearly two dozen prostitutes ended up in court.

"Twenty-two of the most repulsive types of degraded womanhood stood huddled together at the prisoners' bar in the Tombs Police Court yesterday," reported the *New York Times*. Mary Reilley, "the proprietress of the premises," was held on $1,000 bail to appear for trial. In April of the next year the District Attorney brought another indictment against the business as "a disorderly house," or brothel.

In 1888 the pitched roof was removed and a third floor added. The overall appearance was Victorianized with Eastlake-style window lintels, a modestly ornate cornice and a late-Victorian saloon entrance with a corner cast-iron pillar.

From 1891 until 1902, Jeremiah J. Cronin and John Murphy ran a bar here. Then Peter J. Boyle took over the saloon until Prohibition. With the saloon shut down, John Pikel leased "the store and basement" from Margaret C. Hyland on September 27, 1921, the year following the enactment of Prohibition. While he ran the place ostensibly as a restaurant, patrons came for the "cider" and the homemade beer imported from Brooklyn by bootlegger Charlie Brennan.

As the twentieth century progressed, the Water Street neighborhood improved. With the development of the South Street Seaport area starting in 1967, tourists and New Yorkers alike rediscovered what had been a somewhat isolated area.

No. 279 Water Street was renamed The Bridge Café in 1979 when the new owners of the building upgraded the restaurant and bar. Today, inside or out, it is difficult to remember that during the second half of the nineteenth century this neat red wooden building was the haunt of murderers, prostitutes, and thugs.

Although showing its age; the wooden building remains relatively unchanged after two centuries.

ART NOUVEAU *NEW YORK EVENING POST* BUILDING

20 VESEY STREET

When it came to their architecture, staid New Yorkers in the late nineteenth century tended to avoid the avant-garde style of Art Nouveau. From the 1890s until just prior to World War I, Paris filled its boulevards with buildings, even its Metro stations, designed in the sinuous, almost sensuous, curving naturalistic lines of Art Nouveau.

New Yorkers, however, preferred more traditional styles like Beaux Arts. Only a handful of Manhattan buildings such as the 1898 New Era Building at 495 Broadway and the 1903 New Amsterdam Theater on 42nd Street would embrace the revolutionary style.

One of the most striking of these would be the *New York Evening Post* building, a bold expression of the Vienna Secession offshoot of Art Nouveau.

In 1905, Vesey Street across from St. Paul's Churchyard was lined with old stores and loft buildings. The *Evening Post*, under the ownership of Oswald Garrison Villard, purchased Nos. 20, 22, and 24 Vesey as a site for its newest home. The property at No. 20 had been in the hands of the Greenwood family since 1790.

In announcing the new site, the *Evening Post* said on March 3, 1905, "The decision to remain downtown is of especial interest in view of the recent removal of the *Times* and other newspapers uptown. The management believes that for a high-class evening newspaper a downtown location is still essential."

Architect Robert D. Kohn was commissioned to design the new structure, which would house the offices and presses of the *Post* as well as leased offices. On March 2, 1906, Kohn filed plans for the new building for Garrison Realty Company, a concern incorporated specifically for this project.

The building was completed in April 1907, and it was like nothing seen in New York before. Rising thirteen stories above the street, with two full floors below, its steel-framed structure was clad in limestone. Kohn based his design on the Vienna Secession movement, yet produced a totally unique building. Half a century later the New York Landmarks Preservation Commission would note, "The building is particularly interesting because, although Art Nouveau in inspiration, it is not copied from any particular building executed in that style.

Kohn's bold design is unique among Manhattan architecture.

A pensive figure stares down onto Vesey Street.

It is primarily a free expression of the architect's individuality."

Four soaring ten-story piers rise from the sidewalk, accentuating the verticality of the structure. Between them, windows bow outward, giving undulating movement to the façade. But Kohn's visual emphasis was above. Below a tall, shallow copper-sheathed mansard stand four gaunt, oversized limestone sculptures. Representing the "Four Periods of Publicity," two were sculpted by Kohn's wife, Estelle Rumbold Kohn, while the other two were executed by Gutzon Borglum, who would later carve Mount Rushmore. Despite the *Post*'s ungenerous comments a year earlier, the *New York Times* was complimentary of the building on its completion. "The color scheme of the structure is gray and bronze, giving an impression similar to that obtained in some of the new business structures on Fifth Avenue," it said. And the *New York Tribune* called the $500,000 building "an imposing structure."

On the evening of April 13, 1907, the *Evening Post* officially opened its 20 Vesey Street headquarters by hosting a grand dinner and play for all employees—from trustees and editors to office boys—and awarding gold medals and gifts to fourteen employees.

The Home Trust Company was located in the ground-floor space, while the *Evening Post* used the two basement floors and the top four floors. From here the *Post* published not only the newspaper, but also other publications such as the highly popular *Nation*.

Other publishing firms moved in, including Yachting Publishing Company; the Ronald Press Company which printed "books for better business"; the *United States Army and Navy Journal* published by W.C. & F.P. Church; and the *Nautical Gazette*.

Non-publishing tenants included the American Multigraph Company, a manufacturer of printing machinery and parts with a plant in Cleveland; the Benvenue Granite Company; the New York Silicate Book Slate Company, manufacturers of school slates; and the Ironmonger Advertising Agency was here until 1917.

But in 1910 an organization moved in that set a trend for the building throughout the century.

Oswald Garrison Villard's grandfather was abolitionist William Lloyd Garrison. From him the *Evening Post*'s publisher had inherited strong commitments to human and equal rights. Following a race riot in 1908 and persistent lynching throughout the country, Villard and other white liberals including Mary White Ovington, William English Walling, and Dr. Henry Moscowitz organized a public meeting to discuss means to combat racial injustice. The National Association for the Advancement of Colored People was soon born.

Villard subsidized the group's national headquarters in the *Post* building. From here its magazine, *The Crisis*, was published and distributed.

Five floors bow outward, providing additional visual interest and motion.

Later other groups sensitive to equality and social betterment would find offices here, among them the Committee on Fair Play. In 1935 the Committee sought to boycott the Berlin Olympics in protest against Germany's Chancellor, Adolf Hitler. The *New York Times* reported on October 11, 1935, that, "The formation of a nation-wide committee on fair play in sports to oppose the participation of American athletes in the Olympic Games in Berlin next Spring was announced yesterday from the headquarters of the new organization at 20 Vesey Street."

Three years later the American Guild for German Cultural Freedom had its headquarters here, as did the American Council on Public Affairs, who published a 50-page pamphlet, *Five Years of Hitler*, from this building. That same year the International Relief Association, also with offices in the building, published its *Youth Betrayed*, which, on the fifth anniversary of Hitler's rise to power, described young people in Germany under the Reich.

The headquarters of the Catholic Interracial Council was here in the 1940s. By then the *New York Post* had moved on. The Mutual Life Insurance Company owned the building until October 30, 1944, when it was sold to an investing firm.

The forward-thinking Oswald
Garrison Villard

    The building continued throughout the rest of the twentieth century to have a varied tenant list: J. S. Frelinghuysen Corp., one of the oldest insurance brokerage firms in New York, signed a lease in October 1949 after forty years at its former location. In the 1960s, 20 Vesey was home to the Practicing Law Institute and, among others, E.E. Pearce Company, a lumber firm.

    Continuing the building's history of involvement with social issues, 20 Vesey Street became the 9/11 Memorial Preview site as the permanent memorial to the victims of 9/11 was under construction.

    In 1965, despite owner opposition, Robert D. Kohn's magnificent and rare Art Nouveau building at 20 Vesey Street was designated a New York City landmark.

TRIBECA

FEDERAL SURVIVOR,
508 CANAL STREET

GIDEON TUCKER HOUSE,
2 WHITE STREET

ANTHONY ARNOUX HOUSE,
139 GREENE STREET

FEDERAL SURVIVOR

508 CANAL STREET

Canal Park Playhouse

In the 1820s merchant tailor John George Rohr was an industrious man. A German immigrant, he recognized that the rapid development of the Canal Street area—just a few years earlier worthless pastureland called Lispenard's Meadows—would be more profitable than the apparel business.

In 1819 the "canal" down the center of Canal Street (actually, it was more accurately a drainage trench) had been covered over to create a sewer, and Canal Street suddenly became an expansive, 100-foot-wide thoroughfare. The major east-west road was quickly developed with mixed-use structures, most with commercial space on the street level and living quarters above.

Around 1820 Rohr began building near-matching, two-and-a-half-story brick buildings along Greenwich Street on leased Lispenard land, just north of Canal Street. Most likely a relative, also named John Rohr, who was a mason and builder, was responsible for their construction. By 1826 the Rohrs had erected a string of sixteen Federal-style houses on Greenwich Street—five south of Canal Street and eleven north. That year they added two more on the south side of Canal Street, between Greenwich and Washington Streets, numbered 239 and 241. Decades later, in 1860, the houses would be renumbered 506 and 508.

Like the rest of Rohr's houses, No. 241 would have had a store on the first floor and living quarters above. These new homes, however, were three stories tall and Rohr included an unusual cast-iron shop front. The shallow, paneled pilasters supported cast-iron arches that mimicked the arched doorway.

Rohr rented the house at No. 241 to Moses S. Phillips. Three years later, James H. Greenfield opened his china store here and would remain for about three years. In the meantime, Roderick Sedgwick, a merchant doing business at 39 Front Street, leased the upper floors.

In 1840, John G. Rohr sold No. 241 to French-born Joseph Batby, a 36-year-old "ivory-turner." Ten years later Batby and his family—wife Sarah and their four children—were still there. Anthony, their son, who was now 16 years old, was already earning a living as a jeweler.

In 1850, Batby was renting rooms to other families as well. In what must have been crowded conditions were another French immigrant, George H. Denot and his wife, Maria; John and Catherine Flaherty; and the family of Irish-born stonecutter James Sinnot: his wife Mary, their daughter, Catherine, and Mary's mother, Mary Kennedy.

Joseph Batby's heirs sold the property in 1870. Two years later, Henry Wellbrook and his family were living upstairs. On Thursday afternoon, May 9, 1872, burglars broke into the apartment while the family was out. The *New York Times* reported, "The place was ransacked, and $300 worth of wearing apparel and jewelry taken." For a family renting small rooms, the theft was no doubt devastating. The $300 loss would amount to about $5,000 today.

Against all odds, the little house survives nearly two centuries after construction.

Matthew Thompson purchased the property in 1882 and built a one-story adjoining workshop in the rear that covered the back lot. Upstairs the tenant list continued to be a broad mix. Among the renters at the turn of the century was retired police officer Peter Kelly.

Whether Joseph Thompson was a relative of Matthew Thompson is unclear, but by 1908 he and James J. Moran ran their plumbing company, Thompson & Moran, from the commercial space. Thompson lived here as well, and in 1914 he got himself into a bit of trouble.

The 50-year-old plumber had been living on a small motorboat off the north shore of Long Island for about a week in August, perhaps on a sort of vacation. Late on the night of August 14 he gave the residents of Northport a scare. The *New York Times* reported the following day that, "Shortly after midnight this morning he aroused the

The Osbornes carefully melded the twenty-first century with the nineteenth in redoing the upstairs interiors.

village by running through the streets, shouting at the top of his voice, 'Get up, the British are coming.' The police think he is suffering from sunstroke."

In 1941 the ground floor was converted to a restaurant, and in the transformation the wonderful cast-iron shop front was removed. The brick front that replaced the cast iron was, at least, thoughtfully laid in Flemish bond.

Throughout the twentieth century the little brick structure was home to a variety of businesses. Then in 1980, Kipp Osborne and his wife, Margot, purchased the house, rearing their daughter here. For a period they ran "Osborne and Osborne" from street level, designing and building custom-made hardwood furniture. Marketed as "furniture-as-art," each piece was dated, signed, and numbered.

Kipp Osborne then renovated the former commercial space into the Canal Park Playhouse, a theater-cabaret. The upstairs was converted to the Canal Park Inn, a bed and breakfast, which opened in 2011. The four rooms (each named for a former owner or resident) were decorated with a nod to the history of the structure.

Despite the unfortunate loss of the rare and early cast-iron façade on the first floor, the 1826 house retains most of its architectural integrity, resulting in what the Landmarks Preservation Commission calls "a striking reminder of the initial phase of the development of New York City in the years of the early republic."

GIDEON TUCKER HOUSE
2 WHITE STREET

Elsewhere in the city in 1809 houses in the new and fashionable Federal style of architecture were rising. Gideon Tucker, however, preferred the traditional eighteenth-century Dutch style for his residence.

The busy Tucker was a successful businessman and politician, a partner in the Tucker & Ludlum plaster factory, school commissioner, Commissioner of Estimates and Assessments, and an Assistant Alderman. His property, on which his factory sat, was considerable. When White Street was laid out across his land in anticipation of residential development, he built his modest but comfortable home at the end of the block at West Broadway.

No. 2 White Street, in all probability, always had a store on the ground floor with residential space above. Built of brick and wood, it featured the distinctive gambrel roof familiar in the earlier Dutch homes, splayed stone lintels, and handsome prominent dormers.

Despite his substantial wealth, Tucker apparently remained in the unpretentious house until he died in 1845. He left a large amount of real estate, including one plot between the Bowery and Fifth Avenue, from 10th to 12th Street, which sold for $1,250.000.

For decades during the twentieth century, while high-rise office buildings crowded in around it, the White Street building housed a liquor store (by now using the address of 235 West Broadway). In the 1980s a bar, taking its name from the surviving painted glass window signs, opened. "The Liquor Store" prospered for a decade.

Then, in 1990, a mosque nearby opened at 245 West Broadway. Because the state's Alcohol Beverage Control law prohibited the selling of liquor within 200 feet of a house of worship, the bar was notified that its liquor license would be revoked. The mosque, in the meantime, insisted it had no objection to the nearby bars. "We don't dictate other people's behavior," an official said.

Neighbors, however, did have an objection. The Liquor Store completed an expansion in 2005. When the new owners applied for a new liquor license, neighbors,

Above the ground floor the Dutch-style house looks much as it did in 1809.

The old Liquor Store sign remains as the
apparel store adopted it as its name.

frustrated with the many bars in the area, pointed out the tavern's proximity to the mosque. The neighbors won and The Liquor Store closed its doors.

The space was taken over by a J. Crew store which continued to use the name The Liquor Store. It prompted *New York Times* journalist Mike Albo to call it, on September 18, 2008, "A package store for preppies."

No. 2 White Street was designated a New York City Landmark in 1966. Two centuries after construction, Gideon Tucker's quaint little house is in a remarkable state of preservation—the great miracle being that it has survived at all.

ANTHONY ARNOUX HOUSE

139 GREENE STREET

As the fashionable Bond Street area filled with grand Federal period homes for New York's elite, similar residences, but scaled down, were being built to the west. At 139 Greene Street, in 1825, a two-story brick house was completed for Anthony Arnoux, a tailor and apparel merchant. Begun a year earlier, it boasted upscale details affordable by financially comfortable, merchant-class buyers without the extravagances of silver door hinges found on Bond Street.

The white marble stonework stood out against the red brick—carved, paneled lintels, an elegant arched entrance, and a carved stoop. Above the simple cornice two stylish dormers with arched windows below broken pediments pierced the peaked roof.

Sadly abused, the 1825 house still retains an amazing amount of period details.

Arnoux apparently leased the house for nearly a decade. Then in 1834 he moved in with his family. By the time they left in 1860, it would appear that Mrs. Arnoux had died. In 1850 only Anthony Arnoux, his five adult children, and a servant were listed as living there.

The Arnoux family was likely prompted to move because of the declining neighborhood. By now the area was filling with commercial establishments and on Greene Street "disorderly houses," or brothels, were common.

A year after the family left, there was a small fire upstairs when a bed "accidentally caught fire," causing $50 damage. In 1862 the house would be documented as a brothel. In 1867 Patrick and Amelia Whalen owned the building when it was placed on the police department's "black list" as a disorderly house.

On Monday night, September 11, 1867, Officer Forgarty of the 8th Precinct "made a descent upon the premises," according to the *New York Times*. Forgarty arrested the Whalens, along with Emma Hughes, Annie Williams, Ida Nicholson, Celia Frank, Nettie Brown, Nettie Raymond, and Isabella Everman, whom the *Times* tactfully referred to as "inmates."

The Whalens were each charged $500 bail (about $6,000 today) to answer at the Court of General Sessions. The newspaper was apparently not satisfied

A similar Federal house on Greene Street had been converted to a French bakery in 1879.

with the $5 fine each of the prostitutes was charged. The reporter said they "departed from the Court-room apparently not much the worse for Forgarty's raid."

At the time of the raid there were no fewer than a dozen other houses of ill repute on Greene Street. But that would all change within the next two decades. But in the meantime, the influx of French immigrants settling in the area prompted *Scribner's Monthly* to label it "The French Quarter" in November 1879.

"This is the *Quartier Francais* of New York. The commonplace, heterogeneous style of the buildings, and the unswerving rectangular course of the streets are American, but the people are nearly all French. French, too, is the language of the signs over the doors and in the windows; and the population is of the lowest and poorest class. There are swarthy faces which have gladdened in mad grimace over the flames of the Hôtel de Ville and become the hue of copper bronze under the sun of New Caledonia."

The writer said, "Turning down Grand street into Greene one day, with half a dozen steps my friend and I were transported in imagination to France. At No. 95 we descended into a basement, the specialties of which were indicated by the sign over the door: 'Sabots et Galoches—Chaussons de Strasbourg.'"

Even this change to Greene Street would be short-lived. By the 1880s the French immigrants were sharing the area with the millinery trade that was establishing a commercial center in the neighborhood. Anthony Arnoux's once-fine brick home was the headquarters of hatmakers Dutton & Disbrow in 1884. By 1893 Hirsch & Co. was here, a dealer in "furs, skins, hatters' raw stock and fur cuttings."

Another fur dealer, Belt, Butler Co., was in the house in 1909. The firm's advertisement in the December issue of *Farm Journal* announced, "Cash paid for

Raw Furs. As New York is the best fur market in America, we can and do pay highest cash prices for hides of Skunks, Minks, 'Coons, Muskrats, Opossums, Foxes, Badgers, Wolves, Beavers, Otter and all fur-bearing animals. We also pay best prices for GINSENG."

By then, 139 Greene Street was an anachronism. Overshadowed by the tall, Victorian cast-iron loft buildings that made up what today is termed the Cast Iron District, it was starkly out of place. Yet while SoHo became industrial, the little house remained. More or less.

A procession of gritty businesses used the building through the twentieth century. In September 1920, Charles F. Noyes Company leased the building for six years to the Central Fire Office, Inc. It became home to businesses as diverse as rags and wastepaper to trucking.

What interior Federal details survived after the Whalens' disorderly house was closed were now long gone. Mantels, newel posts, and ceiling medallions were gutted for industrial purposes. The fine doorway and sidelights that survived through the 1930s were obliterated for a freight dock—a loading platform erected over the marble stoop. A wide entrance was broken through a parlor window. The abuse of 139 Greene Street led to the Department of Buildings labeling it an "unsafe building" in 1939.

Then in the last half of the century, change came again. SoHo and the Cast Iron District were rediscovered. One-by-one the vintage buildings were restored and recycled into artists' lofts, galleries, and trendy shops.

In the late 1960s, Richard L. Feigen, an art dealer, purchased No. 139. He sold the house in 1973 to Peter W. Ballantine, who intended to restore it as his private home.

Ballantine was faced with an imposing task. While the house, amazingly, retained much of its Federal architectural detailing, it was grossly defaced. The once-fine doorway had been bricked up. The parlor level contained an industrial entrance and the interior was non-existent.

That same year, the New York Landmarks Conservancy listed the house on its "Endangered Buildings" list, mentioning the "ghastly hole to the left of the doorway" and the "disfiguring brick patch beneath the hole." Yet the Conservancy allowed that, "Despite this degradation, much of the Federal character and detailing remains, from the dormers, which are often the first to go on these buildings, to the simple lintels on the second-story windows, and the elegant arch of the front door."

Ballantine began the project in 1974, beginning with the first-floor windows. But the cost of restoration and the restrictions of landmark buildings have made slow going for the rescue of No. 139. Today little progress seems to have been made. But the fact that the dignified reminder of Greene Street's residential past exists at all is amazing.

CHINATOWN

EDWARD MOONEY HOUSE, 18 BOWERY

LOEW'S CANAL STREET THEATRE
31 CANAL STREET

14TH WARD INDUSTRIAL SCHOOL,
256 - 258 MOTT STREET

CALVERT VAUX'S 14TH WARD INDUSTRIAL SCHOOL

256–258 MOTT STREET

John Jacob Astor III was interested in making money. His wife, Charlotte, was interested in spreading it around—much of it going to her favorite charities. As *The Cyclopaedia of American Biography* stated in 1898, "He furnished the money; she distributed it."

In mid-nineteenth-century New York the squalid Five Points section of the city teemed with waifs known as "street arabs"—the orphaned or abandoned children of prostitutes, drug addicts, and alcoholics— who fended for themselves. In response, the Children's Aid Society was formed in 1853 to "ensure the physical and emotional well being of children and families." Charlotte Astor embraced the cause. *The Cyclopaedia of American Biography* said, "She expended not only large sums, but personal energy and sympathy on behalf of the poor of New York, contributing thousands of dollars to the Children's Aid Society."

In its early days, the Society sponsored "The Orphan Train Movement," whereby school-age boys were sent off to the American West to work for settlers on their farms. Townspeople would inspect the boys, select those who appeared to be able to do a decent day's work, and take them home. There were no adoption proceedings, no birth certificates involved, and the boys received no pay other than room and board. While abolitionists decried the practice as a form of slavery, others like Mrs. Astor insisted the boys were escaping a much worse fate on the streets of Manhattan. Every Christmas she spent about $2,000 to send one hundred orphans westward.

The Society also provided lodging houses for newsboys and bootblacks—charging six cents a night for a bed, a hot meal, a bath, and a sermon. Once a year the children were entertained with a "Summer Festival" complete with the crowning of the Queen of May and numerous "addresses"; proof, according to the *New York Times*, that the Children's Aid Society "at least have not forgotten that 'the poor we have always with us.'"

Charlotte Astor died of cancer in 1887 after decades of supporting the Society. John Jacob Astor was determined to memorialize her by building a new "Industrial School" in the impoverished Italian 14th Ward neighborhood. Rather than simply shipping the indigent children off to the West, the school would teach them the fundamental skills necessary to make a living at home. Astor purchased the lot at 256–258 Mott Street for $21,000 and hired Calvert Vaux to design the school.

Vaux produced a visually entertaining Victorian Gothic structure of red Pennsylvania brick with terra-cotta and brownstone trim. Brick buttresses and a pointed Gothic entranceway drew attention upward to the stepped Dutch gable. Finished in 1888, the school building cost Astor $42,000, just under $1 million in today's dollars. Rising four stories above the street, it included a "roomy basement" with a kitchen and separate dining rooms for teachers and students. The first floor housed kindergarten and primary classrooms, the second and third floors contained classrooms for older children, and the top floor housed rooms for primary and industrial schoolwork. A playground was located in the rear.

While Vaux's design was mainly Victorian Gothic, he gave a nod to New York's Dutch roots with a stepped gable.

In the main hallway a brass tablet read:
> *This building has been erected in affectionate*
> *remembrance of*
> *Mrs. Charlotte Augusta Astor*
> *by her husband.*
> *John Jacob Astor*
> *New York 1888*

Above the entrance a carved plaque announces the name of the school.

Upon the school's dedication, the *New York Times* said, "The memorial to Mrs. Astor will form an attractive centre of industry, thrift and cleanliness in a region which is noted for none of those characteristics." The article described the neighborhood as "a district of wretchedness, poverty and squalor."

In Astor's monument to his charitable wife, the underprivileged learned their future trades well into the twentieth century. Today the population of the neighborhood is more Chinese than Italian, and the building has been converted to cooperative apartments. The ground-floor façade is stained with the attempts to remove graffiti; however, the integrity of Calvert Vaux's 14th Ward Industrial School shines through.

LOEW'S CANAL STREET THEATRE

31 CANAL STREET

During the first quarter of the twentieth century, the impoverished population on the Lower East Side could escape the squalid conditions that surrounded them in two places: the majestic churches and the sumptuous movie palaces.

Marcus Loew was born into this neighborhood in 1870. The son of Jewish immigrants, he worked his way up from a newsboy to owning his own newspaper and selling furs. When he met fellow furrier Adolph Zukor, the direction of his life would take a turn.

Around the turn of the century the pair established the Automatic Vaudeville Company and opened penny arcades with hand-cranked "motion picture" vignettes. As projection moving pictures developed, Loew began purchasing established theaters and renovating them into motion picture houses. Before long he was erecting his own buildings; one of which, the Loew's Avenue B Theatre, was on the site of the tenement in which he grew up.

As the motion picture industry matured, feature-length films developed and movie theaters expanded into lavish temples dedicated to film. In January 1926, Loew's company contracted architect Thomas Lamb to design a theater at 31 Canal Street. Lamb

The exquisite terra cotta façade above street level remains a show-stopper.

Lamb combined Baroque exuberance with Regency elegance in a happy if unexpected marriage of styles.

had already established himself as a theater designer, and for this one he produced an ornate terra-cotta palace, completed in 1927.

Approximately four stories tall, the façade was embellished with griffins, urns, festoons, and garlands—a marriage of Regency elegance with Baroque abundance. The moviegoer would pass through the relatively narrow 22-foot-wide Canal Street entrance and lobby into a 2,314-seat auditorium—the second-largest motion picture theater in the city. The interior space was decorated with lush terra-cotta ornamentation and grand chandeliers.

While the Canal Street Theatre was a fixture in the neighborhood, it never showed the premier films that were relegated to the more visible Times Square theaters. Here "B" comedies, westerns, and serials played to masses of local residents before the advent of television. It was here, though, on April 17, 1940, that Eddie Cantor's *Forty Little Mothers* premiered.

The last movie was screened here in the late 1950s, and Loew's Canal Street Theatre locked the doors for good. After the building was sold in 1960, the lobby was used as a retail store and the seats were removed from the sumptuous auditorium to make room for warehouse space.

The once-grand Loew's Canal Street Theatre, now a tawdry retail outlet for electronics, sat unnoticed until 2010, when owner Thomas Sung supported a feasibility study to convert the theater into a multipurpose performance arts center.

That year, the Committee to Revitalize and Enrich the Arts and Tomorrow's Economy (CREATE) was granted $150,000 from the Lower Manhattan Development Corporation to conduct the study. That same year, both the façade and interior were granted landmark designation by the New York City Landmarks Preservation Commission.

Today, while residents wait to see what will become of the once-proud theater, dust continues to settle on the chandeliers hanging over crates of electronics. The ornate terra-cotta detailing that once dazzled immigrant moviegoers remains in an astounding state of preservation.

EDWARD MOONEY HOUSE
18 BOWERY

Life was good for James DeLancey during the British rule of New York. He owned an estate in Westchester County, property in Manhattan, and a farm north of the city. His problems started with the American Revolution.

Wanting to cover all his bets and unsure of which side would win the conflict, DeLancey straddled the political fence. He secured a seat in the New York Assembly in 1768 by winning the support of the Sons of Liberty, who rallied against British control. In the meantime, however, he was rubbing shoulders with the Crown, meeting secretly and assuring his loyalty. That all ended when in February 1775 he was exposed as a British loyalist in the legislature. By May he had left New York never to return.

On March 6, 1777, the Provincial Congress appointed Commissioners to "take into their custody & possession all the personal property" of loyalists with ten days' notice. The families were allowed to keep their clothing, a few pieces of furniture, and three months' provisions. Everything else was sold at public auction. Things got worse for the loyalists when, on October 22, 1779, the Congress passed "An Act for the forfeiture and sale of the estates of those who have adhered to the enemies of this state." Loyalists were banned from the state under penalty of death "without benefit of Clergy."

When the Commissioners of Forfeiture auctioned off DeLancey's property in 1785, estimated at $50,000 (several million in today's dollars), Edward Mooney was there. A high-profile player in the colonial wholesale meat business, he was also the representative of the city butchers in the Society of Mechanics and Tradesmen. He purchased the empty lot at the corner of Bowery and Pell for his new residence.

Mooney built his house sometime between the auction date, just after the British fled New York, and 1789, the year Washington was inaugurated on Wall Street. The completed red-brick structure displayed elements of the newer Federal style of architecture while holding on to some traditional Georgian designs. A fanlight with delicate spiderweb tracery graced the deeply set arched Georgian doorway.

On either side were slender columns. The double keystone over the entrance was repeated in the stone window lintels.

Edward Mooney lived in his house until his death in 1800. Seven years later, its size was doubled by an addition to the rear. By the 1820s the house had been converted to a tavern, and was never again to be used as a private residence. Its many transformations would include a hotel, pool room, brothel, retail store, restaurant, and a Chinese club.

Through it all, the exterior of the house remained virtually unaltered, save for the unfortunate green metal entrance door seen today. Between the paired chimneys on the Pell Street side, an arched window with its original eighteenth-century mullions survives, flanked by two quarter-round windows. Inside, beneath the handsome gambrel roof, the hand-sawn timbers can be seen. A few interior details original to the house, including window trims and frames, and the oval-shaped handrail on the staircase in the 1807 addition, remain.

Other than the unfortunate replacement doors, the entrance is amazingly intact—including the spidery fan light.

The sole surviving townhouse from the time of the Revolution, the Edward Mooney house stands in a much-changed neighborhood. Once a quiet street of eighteenth-century homes, this is now part of New York's bustling Chinatown.

The rare Colonial survivor was restored in 1971 and today houses a bank._

The Mooney House miraculously survives—a Colonial relic in the midst of bustling Chinatown.

CAPTAIN WOOD HOUSE,
310 SPRING STREET

EMMA LAZARUS HOUSE,
18 WEST 10TH STREET

ASCH BUILDING
23-29 WASHINGTON PLACE

GREENWICH VILLAGE

VILLAGE CIGARS
AND THE MYSTERY MOSAIC
CHRISTOPHER STREET
AND SEVENTH AVENUE

TWIN PEAKS
102 BEDFORD STREET

THE PEPPER POT INN
146 WEST 4TH STREET

CAPTAIN WOOD HOUSE

310 SPRING STREET

On the south side of Spring Street, near Greenwich Street, an abused red-brick building of little apparent interest sits among its industrial neighbors. However, this house, the former home of a sea captain and just shy of two centuries old, has plenty of stories to tell.

The seafaring Dennison Wood married 17-year-old Lydia McKildo in 1804, while he was still a ship's mate working on vessels bringing sugar to New York. By 1807 he had invested with at least one partner in his own sloop, the *Cornelia*, which sailed back and forth from the city to St. Thomas.

Before long Trinity Church began development of what had been known as Trinity Farm—an expansive tract of land stretching north towards Greenwich Village. Wood and his wife were living on Greenwich Street when, in October 1818, he purchased the nearby lot at 282 Spring Street from Trinity Church for $1,400—about $25,000 today.

The site was a logical choice for Wood. It sat just a few blocks from the river front in a burgeoning area of new homes and businesses. Their wide Federal-style home was completed within the year.

Like most others in the area, the two-story house was wood-framed and clad in Flemish-bond brick. Paneled brownstone lintels capped the windows, and prim dormers sat above a modest cornice.

Dennison Wood spent much of his time at sea. In 1819 he was captain of the brig *Levant*, owned by Hall & Hoyt. The ship carried goods to and from Savannah. By 1824 he captained a larger ship, the *Louisa Matilda*, after Hall & Hoyt partnered with James & Cornelius Seguine to form the Established Line.

He sailed regularly from New York to Savannah for about two decades. In the 1830s Wood commanded the *Tybee*, which transported not only goods, but also passengers. An advertisement in the *New York Evening Post* listed the *Tybee* among "vessels of the first class—their accommodations for passengers are extensive and well furnished; they sail very fast and their commanders are men of capability and experience."

In 1837 Dennison Wood was captain of the *Trenton*, a 427-ton ship that also sailed between New York and Savannah. His extensive time away from home did not deter

Dennison from fathering nine children, who were raised in the house on Spring Street.

By the time of his death, apparently in 1846, Wood had fallen on hard times. That year creditors auctioned off the house; but the family, unwilling to have Lydia removed from her home, pooled their money to save it. Son-in-law Samuel C. Brown, a merchant, purchased the house, and the following year transferred it to a trust of family members all of whom had contributed funds.

Lydia, now 60 years old, was given residential life rights while the family rented out a portion of the structure to offset the expenses. The trust's contract stipulated that upon Lydia's death the house would be sold and the proceeds distributed among the partners: George Bucknam, William A. Wood, Dennison B. Wood, and Samuel C. Brown.

Esteemed artist Rembrandt Peale painted Dennison Wood's portrait.

To accommodate the rental portion, a third floor was added in 1847, along with a storefront. While the brickwork of the third-story addition was not in Flemish bond, care was taken to match the paneled lintels and other architectural elements so that the renovation was nearly seamless. Along with Lydia and her son Dennison, boarders would occupy the upper floors.

The following year the address was renumbered to No. 310 Spring Street.

Downstairs James Haydock opened his small dry goods store and would remain for over two decades. Among the boarders were Catharine Wainwright and her husband, William. Daughters Mary and Emma lived here as well. Both were teachers and Mary earned $275 at Public School No. 3 at Hudson and Grove Street. Tragedy struck on May 1, 1865, when William committed suicide by "shooting himself through the head...in a room at his dwelling No. 310 Spring-street," as reported in the *New York Times* the following day.

Fifty-four-year-old Dennison B. Wood was appointed an election pool inspector in October of that year. Sadly, he died a few weeks later on Friday, November 3. There was no space in the converted Spring Street house for a funeral, so it was held at the residence of a friend, W. S. Fogg at 431 West 22nd Street.

In 1869, Thomas Courtney's dry goods store replaced James Haydock's. Within the year Courtney, an Irish immigrant, moved his family in upstairs. With him lived his wife, Mary, and their three children.

That same year John Coughlin was rooming here. The unscrupulous boarder also went by the name of John Taylor. Police arrested him after finding hidden in his room suitcases and trunks which he had stolen from city hotels.

Lydia Wood died in 1873 at the age of 86 years, bringing to a close 54 years of Wood family residency at 310 Spring Street.

The once mostly residential neighborhood had greatly changed by now. The streets were filled with shops catering to the shipping trade, and disreputable saloons flourished near the waterfront. In 1875, Courtney's dry goods store caught fire, damaging the building and wiping out most of the merchant's inventory. Insurance covered the full $200 worth of damage to the structure and, most likely, the storefront that remains today was installed during the reparations.

As the repairs were being made, Samuel Brown, acting as trustee, sold the building to John H. Heaselden for $11,500—nearly $200,000 today. Although Heaselden was a liquor dealer, he continued to lease the store to Courtney and rent out the rooms upstairs.

Yet again, not all of the boarders proved upstanding. On the cold winter morning of January 11, 1878, "at an early hour" according to the *New York Times*, roomer William Stanley was up to no good.

The 23-year-old locomotive engineer was lured by the goods in the shop below. Courtney's store was protected by an iron gate; but that would not be enough to stop Stanley. He broke off the padlock, smashed a pane of glass, and crawled in.

Perhaps a bit too greedy, the young thief gathered up "a large quantity of goods, consisting of 6 pairs of blankets, 36 shirts, 23 pairs of drawers, 1 cardigan jacket, 1 coat, 18 neck shawls, 10 skirts, and 23 pairs of woolen socks, altogether worth $93, and decamped with them," reported the newspaper.

The unwieldy amount of goods caught the eye of Officer Kiernan of the 8th Precinct, who promptly arrested the man.

In an attempt to prevent further burglaries, Courtney hired Charles Fisher to sleep in the store. On a Sunday night in early November 1879 the watchman awoke to find he was not alone. Two men were standing near his cot. William Nichols, a machinist from Boston, and William Johnson, a New York boatman, had squeezed through the aperture for the fanlight over the front door.

Police heard Fisher's calls before the men had a chance to make off with anything.

Despite the repeated attempts at theft, Courtney's business thrived. In 1884 he expanded the store space to the rear. Architect L. Sibley designed a single-story addition that nearly doubled the commercial space. Within four years Courtney brought his son, Thomas, Jr., into the business, proudly renaming the store

Thomas Courtney & Son.

Courtney raised the wrath of eminent thread manufacturer George A. Clark & Brother when he began undercutting other retailers. Courtney was selling Clark's "O.N.T." spool cotton at four cents per spool, or 48 cents per dozen, significantly lower than the market price. Clark's sent a letter to its distributors that read in part, "In the interest of trade prices, we urgently request that you decline to fill orders, either directly or indirectly, for Clark's 'O.N.T.' spool cotton" from Thomas Courtney.

Courtney's was still here in 1939, advertising "Headlight Overalls."

In 1897 the *Times* noted that "Mrs. Hannah Heaselden" had sold "a three-story brick tenement with store." The buyer was Thomas Courtney. After nearly three decades of living and doing business from No. 310, the building was now his. The merchant added a cast-iron pediment above the cornice that announced "COURTNEY'S." The pediment would survive for nearly a century.

Although the Courtney family moved to West 11th Street within a few years, the business remained on Spring Street. At the turn of the century, reflecting the change in the neighborhood, the former dry goods store was now listed as "working men's clothes." Expanding the business, the Courtneys adapted a portion of the building as an apparel sewing room, listing "shirtmakers" in the telephone directory in 1904.

Part of the ground floor space was leased to John Gallagher, who ran a small blacksmith shop here. In the meantime, boarders continued to live in the upper floors. Among them, in 1909, were 25-year-old Mary H. E. Driscoll, who worked in the shirtmaking shop and was clerk "for a dry goods store," most probably Courtney's; and the McCarthy sisters: Nora, the foreperson of a laundry; and Julia, who worked as a clerk in a publishing firm.

On September 29, 1909, a small article in the *New York Times* probably raised more than a few eyebrows. The blacksmith, John Gallagher, had died. He left his entire estate, valued at $10,000, to Mary Driscoll, "a young woman employed by a firm of shirtmakers having a factory above his shop." The article made special note that "He makes no mention in his will of a sister, niece and other relatives."

In 1928, while Driscoll and the McCarthy sisters lived on here, another shady tenant moved in. Julian Alarciz was arrested on May 26 for attempting to pick the pockets of sleeping persons in the interborough subway and elevated stations.

Decades later Charles McCarthy joined his female relatives here around 1947. When Thomas Courtney, Jr., died, the business closed. In 1950, No. 310 Spring Street was sold to Mary Driscoll and the McCarthys for $6,000.

The new owners found a tenant: Bell Maintenance Company, designers and manufacturers of neon signs, moved in.

Mary Driscoll, the same young woman who had made shirts for Thomas Courtney in 1909, was still living in the house a half century later in 1957. That year on December 21 the 75-year-old woman ventured out during a ferocious wind storm. "Shortly before 8 p.m.—at the height of the storm," reported the *New York*

Thomas Courtney's Victorian storefront remains, somewhat altered.

Times, she "was struck and killed by an automobile as she was crossing from the north to the south side of Canal Street at Greenwich Street."

Nora McCarthy lived on here until her death in the 1960s. Her executors sold the house to Bronx residents Theodore and Norma Mass for $25,000 in 1967. Bell Maintenance Company moved out that year. The commercial space on the ground floor remained vacant for nine years, while renters continued to live upstairs.

Unity Environmental Corp. purchased the building in 1989. For a period the first floor became a small restaurant, the Bell Caffe, while the upper rooms continued on as residential spaces.

Today Captain Dennison Wood's home is more than a bit careworn. The nineteenth-century storefront of Thomas Courtney remains, slightly altered, and, astoundingly, the entrance door survives. But with a little imagination one can be transported to a time in the 1820s when a ship's captain returned home to his family here after weeks at sea.

THE QUIRKY 'TWIN PEAKS'

102 BEDFORD STREET

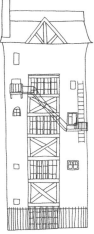

In the spring of 1925, millionaire Otto Kahn had lunch in a most unexpected spot—the tiny wooden tearoom named the Little House on Greenwich Village's Bedford Street. Joining him was builder Clifford Reed Daily, who lived nearby on Sheridan Square. Daily was pitching a deal.

Behind the Little House sat the venerable three-story townhouse at 102 Bedford. A frame building sitting on a brick basement, it had been constructed around 1830, when Greenwich Village was experiencing a population and building boom.

By the turn of the century, it was owned by real estate investor Richard Bogardus, who, judging from the fire escape he installed in 1901, rented the property to more than one family. After his death his estate kept the house for some years before selling it to "an investor" in 1913.

When Daily met Kahn for lunch, he gave an impassioned plea for financial backing for his "dream" that revolved around the old wooden house next door.

"I am only a dreamer," he said to the financier, "and this is my dream."

During the first decades of the twentieth century, Greenwich Village was New York's Bohemia—its winding streets peopled by artists, musicians, and poets. But Daily felt that their creativity was stifled by a restricting environment. He envisioned a fanciful structure of angles and half-timbering, of dormers and balconies—a place that could set the imagination free.

The *New York Times* quoted Daily on May 18, 1926: "It is just as easy to build beautiful things and it is a lot easier to rent them. We are being herded into barracks, one the same as the next. The result is that the village is growing into a desert of mediocrity, with nothing of inspiration to the villagers, who depend a great deal on their surroundings for the inspiration that comes." Daily intended to do his part to rectify the situation. He purchased 102 Bedford Street that same year and, with his grand dreams and Otto Kahn's money in hand, set out on a $14,000 renovation.

A year later, the transformation was completed. According to building records there were two "non-housekeeping" apartments per floor—a total of ten that rented for $68.50 a month. The house was now five stories tall, slathered in stucco, with two steep gables. Tiny dormers and pretend balconies projected from the medieval-looking structure, creating what the *AIA Guide to New York City* would later call "pure Hansel and Gretel."

Clifford Daily christened his dream house "Twin Peaks."

Although *National Geographic Traveler* contends that, "Otto Kahn remodeled the building after one in Nuremberg," it seems that the whimsical design was more likely based solely in Daily's imagination.

On May 21, 1926, the building was dedicated. And what a dedication it was. The *New York Times* remarked, "One of the dreams that are nurtured in Greenwich Village, usually to become nothing more than dreams, will attain reality with the dedication of Twin Peaks." Here, the newspaper said, "In this apartment building are centered the ambitions of the life and time of Clifford Reed Daily."

In a ceremony deemed by the *Times* to be "novel exercises," screen actress Mabel Normand christened the house by smashing a bottle of champagne from a platform erected on the roof. Holy water was sprinkled on the building and acorns were burned to honor Pan by the Princess Amelia Troubetzkoy, an American writer who had been married to a Russian prince prior to the Revolution.

Clifford Reed Daily's fanciful dreams crashed a year later when he turned the property over to Otto Kahn in foreclosure. Interestingly, the millionaire Kahn's daughter lived here for a period alongside other tenants of more meager financial means.

Silent screen actress Mabel Normand christened the building from one of the gables.

As if plucked from a fairy tale, Clifford Daily's dream house charms passersby nearly a century later.

The arcane entrance is accessed through a skinny side door.

The apartments were charming, with odd angles and quirky amenities, yet their small size—most only about 20 by 18 feet—makes questionable the local legends that Douglas Fairbanks, Jr., and Walt Disney lived here.

In the mid-1980s architect Stephen J. Kagel purchased Twin Peaks for $350,000, converting it to co-op apartments. In June 1998 the co-op owners put it back on the market for $2.5 million. The eccentric structure remains a monument to Clifford Reed Daily's quixotic dream of nearly a century ago.

THE PEPPER POT INN

146 WEST 4TH STREET

The elegant brick Federal-style homes that lined Washington Square were by the mid-1830s spilling on to the side streets. One such house rose at 146 West 4th Street, just half a block from the park towards Sixth Avenue. Three and a half stories high over a deep English basement, it featured a refined, arched entrance with a delicate fanlight. The red brick was accented with white stone, similar to its high-toned neighbors on the park. In 1871 owner J. J. Lyons added a full fourth floor and a gently sloped roof, which his building permit generously deemed "a mansard roof."

By 1915 the streets once busy with the landaus and coupes of the wealthy saw the first horseless carriages. The wealthiest residents had moved further north and Greenwich Village was drawing poets, artists, and musicians to its quaint and rambling streets. It was a time of enormous change and the nation was fascinated with a new mode of entertainment: the motion picture.

New York was the epicenter of the silent movie industry and one couple, Dr. Carlyle Sherlock and his wife, Viola, tried their hand at acting. In 1915, Carlyle played the part of Paul Greer in *The Stain of Dishonor*. The 23-year-old Viola acted in a handful of productions. But before long they would abandon the silent screen for another endeavor.

In 1918, Carlyle Sherlock purchased No. 146 West 4th Street and renovated it as a restaurant-nightclub, the Pepper Pot Inn. A later promotion would say it was "established by Dr. Carlyle

A postcard shows the still-surviving Federal style doorway around 1920.

The ceiling of the dining room, below street level, was strung with chili peppers and paper lanterns.

Sherlock for his wife, Viola, when they retired from the Motion Picture Screen, as a meeting place for their friends of the Motion Picture, Theatrical, Bridge and Chess World." (Even more than acting, chess was the passion of "Doc" Sherlock.)

The former English basement, a few steps below street level, became a restaurant where "Vi" served her homemade cakes, pies, and puddings. A postcard would boast, "The chickens and eggs come from 'Air Castle Acres,' Viola Sherlock's 300-acre Orange County estate. The special blend of coffee is percolated and then filtered through Japanese rice paper; the Chili Con Carne is done in real Mexican style; the Virginia Ham, and other Southern Dishes specially prepared by our old Southern chef."

The parlor and second story of the old house became dance floors. And while the Sherlocks rented rooms in the house directly across the street at 145 West 4th, Carlyle reserved the top floor for Viola's private studio, "the largest in the village." Flooded with sunlight from the expansive studio windows, the space was decorated in true Edwardian style, with wicker furniture, Chinese lanterns, and palms.

On the third floor was the Bridge Room. The space was rented for private banquets and meetings and soon became home to Frank Marshall's chess club. Marshall had held the title of United States chess champion since 1909, and the club attracted professional and amateur chess players nationwide. On September 24, 1920, for instance, the *Evening World* announced, "The chess champion of the United States, Frank J. Marshall, will begin tonight a series of exhibitions of simultaneous play, playing a score or more of experts at once, at the Pepper Pot, the Greenwich Village chess divan conducted by Dr. Sherlock... Mr. Marshall and Dr. Sherlock will also play a match at 'Kriegslpiel,' a chess game in which each player moves without knowing the moves of his opponent." The exhibitions were given every Friday evening and "will be witnessed and participated in by many of the strongest players in the Greater City."

The Pepper Pot was a sensation. Entertainers like Al Jolson stopped in and neighborhood artists made it home. Waitresses, or "hostesses," were often music or art students from nearby New York University. But it was the bohemian atmosphere as much as the good food that drew the crowds. "The uniqueness and originality, the environment and bonhomie, all serve to make you remember the Pepper Pot when you are away from it and you long to return," said an advertisement. "It gets into your heart,

The top floor became Viola Sherlock's private refuge.

too, and you will never be able to lose the magic of it all the days of your life." *Theatre Magazine* called it "the realest thing in Bohemian atmosphere" in the country.

On the tables of the restaurant were candles—actually globs of wax created by innumerable melted candles—inspired by the Pepper Pot Club in London. The first candles were lit in a glass tumbler. When the initial candle was melted down, another was added, and then another. Before long a tall, volcano-looking mountain of wax resulted, some up to four feet tall. Visiting artists would often sit and carve sculptures out of the waxen mound—temporary works of art that would soon be covered in dripping wax.

A writer from *Theatre Magazine* in 1922 described her visit: "We found 'The Pepper Pot' jammed... that is the main room, several steep steps down from the street level. And it had all the earmarks of your true Bohemia... low ceilings... candle-light... a pleasingly irregular shape fitted with nooks and corners and wooden seats along the walls." The writer, Angelina, noted a large table in the center of the room. "This table was filled with young artists and newspaper men, we were told, and every few minutes someone jumped up from it and went to the piano and played... popular stuff, but with a nice feeling for the soft pedal and a full extraction of the rhythm."

Angelina then noticed Metropolitan Opera star Sophie Braslau in one corner, and Chicago Opera tenor Signor Ciccolini at another table. Soprano Marguerita Sylva was there with her aviator husband, Major Smith. The diva said to Angelina, "Isn't this the most interesting place!"

The 1920s would bring two major forces to New York and the Pepper Pot: Prohibition and jazz.

Like many of the nightclubs of Manhattan, the Pepper Pot managed to continue business almost-as-usual despite Prohibition. Patrons still managed to have wine or

Young hostesses, often students, pose in the garden.

drinks with dinner—and only occasionally did the Sherlocks have to answer for it.

But there was that problem of jazz.

In the days before air conditioning, open windows let in the night breezes but also let out the blaring music. Inside the Pepper Pot flappers in fringed dresses danced the Charleston and the Black Bottom with college boys. The Roaring Twenties had arrived and the neighbors were not pleased.

On February 11, 1921, two women from across the street—Mrs. Hollis B. Page of No. 143 West 4th Street and the Sherlocks' landlady, Mrs. Alberting de Creveling of No. 145—filed a complaint with Magistrate Corrigan in the Jefferson Market Court.

Mrs. De Creveling complained, "We can get no sleep. Something has got to be done with these coal mines, these diamond mines, these gold mines and—that Pepper Pot at No. 144 W. 4th Street, directly opposite our homes." When she insinuated that the restaurant sold liquor, the magistrate asked, "Do you mean intoxicating?"

She replied, "Why, our young girls and boys are picked up unconscious from the stuff they receive at these places."

After calling the patrons "slum seekers," she turned her attention to the noise. "That jazz music—oh, my! Those funny ditties that they play on the phonograph. I need sleep."

Carlyle Sherlock arrived in court before the magistrate on February 17. He was armed and ready.

"Mrs. Creveling says realty values have depreciated in Greenwich Village because of the foreign element," he said. "I rent my apartment from her. A year ago I paid $25 a month, and now my rent has been jacked up to $125 a month. Realty may have depreciated, but rents in the Village have not."

The *Evening World* reported, "The proprietor had on hand a number of witnesses and other evidence to show the place is so quiet chess players make it a headquarters." The charge of "conducting a noisy place and public nuisance" was dismissed.

Jazz continued on West 4th Street, even finding its way to the third-floor chess club. On March 14, 1922, the *Evening World* reported that players "even get up in the midst of a game, it is alleged, and change a gambit into a gambol, gaily seizing

In what had been a dignified parlor in the 1830s,
flappers danced the Charleston in the 1920s.

their partners about the waist and tripping all around the place under the inspiration of a jazz band." The newspaper described the Pepper Pot saying, "It is extremely Greenwich Village—with an automatic piano in the candle-lit basement and a group of furious jazzers two floors above."

A year later Viola, now 28 years old, would be arrested along with two customers by Patrolman Joseph Reilly. Harry Maunbach was a 33-year-old artist from Chicago who was having dinner with a Brooklyn blueprint maker, 25-year-old Walker Wacke. "The patrolman testified in Essex Market Court yesterday that he found some liquor at a table occupied by Maunbach and Wacke in the restaurant," reported the *New York Times* on January 15, 1923. The trio was held on $500 bail each.

Nineteen-year-old Adelaide Miller was in charge of the checkroom on the evening of December 19, 1925, when 70 sophomores from City College were holding a smoker in the Bridge Room. What started out as a normal night turned into anything but that when 200 freshmen rushed in and started a riot.

"Four or five hundred additional guests were directly or indirectly drawn into the turmoil, and pottery, silverware and chair legs, according to the police, were used by the combatants," said the *New York Times*.

In the melee, Adelaide was knocked down and received cuts and bruises. Several of the gang broke into Viola's upstairs studio, "breaking several rare Egyptian vases and leaving the place in confusion," the newspaper reported. Despite reserves from the Mercer Street police station being called in, no arrests were made.

At the same time that Adelaide Miller was checking coats, 28-year-old Gerold Schrage worked a few nights a week singing and playing piano. The classically trained pianist came from Aberdeen, Washington, and tried in vain to launch a concert tour.

The *Times* noted that, "Schrage's tenor voice was much admired in the Village, where he sang at numerous parties of friends. It was said, however, that his subjects—invariably classical—frequently were 'over the heads' of his listeners, and that his efforts to entertain consequently often 'fell-flat.'" Jazz was not in his repertoire.

The young entertainer lived in a second-floor room at 289 West 12th Street nearby. Things were going all right until his mother sent word that she was coming for a visit in June 1926. Schrage panicked, realizing that his mother would find out that he was not working as a classical pianist, but as a nightclub entertainer.

"I cannot bear the thought of her learning that I am a cabaret singer," he told friends.

A week before his mother's scheduled arrival, Schrage left the Pepper Pot and returned to his room. He ripped his bed sheets, stuffing the fabric into the crevices of the doors. Newspaper and strips of cloth were pushed into the keyholes and cracks along the windows. He then turned on the gas jets.

By the time his landlady, Veronica Flanagan, smelled the odor of gas and the door was broken down, the young man was dead.

Greenwich Village was still the center of art in the 1930s, and Washington Square became an impromptu outdoor gallery in 1932. But winter weather threatened to end the struggling artists' exhibitions. "Doc" Sherlock came to their rescue by offering two floors of the Pepper Pot as an indoor, year-round gallery. By December 9, 50 of what the *Times* called "needy artists" had taken advantage of the offer. About 300 oil paintings, watercolors, and etchings were hung here to be admired—and bought—by patrons.

Exactly a year later, on December 5, 1933, Prohibition was repealed. Finally New Year's Eve could be rung in with a toast. On January 1, 1934, the *Times* said, "The lid was off last night in the city's hundreds of hotels, restaurants and night clubs. Not since the beginning of the dry era fourteen years ago was there so great a New Year's crowd as that which turned out to greet 1934." The newspaper reported on the cost of the celebration in the Village. "At the Pepper Pot, liquor-licensed, the charge was $10 a couple, with a bottle of wine and dinner."

By 1938 the Sherlocks had retired to their country home and Harry Shecter took over the Pepper Pot. The *New York Times* described the club "which boasts it is the Village's oldest night spot and certainly has been in business a lot of years." The newspaper said it had "a certain feeling as of the old speakeasy days, dim lights, intimate surroundings, a small dance floor, no regular show but an m.c. (Boyd Heathen) who sings. Also, Works of Art on the walls, a fortuneteller and, over in one corner, the patriarchal John Henry Titus, author of one version of 'The Face on the Bar Room Floor'; if not Mr. Titus, then another neighborhood celebrity, of whom there have been many in the proud Pepper Pot past. It is that kind of place, and it gets livelier as the evening goes on."

The club now had "the famed Voodoo Room, which is a sort of Greenwich Village version of Small's Paradise in Harlem." Here were singing waiters, a tap dancer named Little Baby Bangs, "songstresses who dispense the torch, sophisticated and rowdy-dow," and the hostess, Dotty Keane, whom the *Times* thought "attractive and courteous."

The Pepper Pot, once the most popular eating place in the Village and a nationwide destination, would not last forever. In 1965 there was still a bar and restaurant in the basement and first floor; but the upper floors had been renovated into apartments. The 1830s Federal-style entrance had been obliterated for a modern, nondescript doorway.

Where jazz music once played, an illicit after-hours club called the New Showcase was run by the Mafia family of Carlo Gambino.

The elegant Federal doorway is gone and the Pepper Pot, once the scene of gaiety and dancing, is home to a vintage clothing store.

Federal and NYPD officers shut it down on July 18, 1971, in a predawn raid.

Today, all traces of Viola and Carlyle's jazz-age nightclub are gone. The upper floors have been renovated into luxury co-ops and the Pepper Pot's dining room below sidewalk level is now the Campus Laundry & Cleaners. One floor above, where young girls with bobbed hair and rolled-down hose danced to the annoyance of neighbors, the Beauty Jewel Spa offers laser skin care.

EMMA LAZARUS HOUSE
18 WEST 10TH STREET

In 1854 the Wall Street banking firm of Winslow, Lanier & Co. had made millionaires of its principals. A senior member of the firm was James Winslow, whose wife, Margaret, was the daughter of partner James F. D. Lanier. The West 10th Street block between Fifth and Sixth Avenues was, at the time, becoming more and more fashionable as the mansions of New York's wealthiest citizens crept northward along Fifth Avenue. Many of the street's earlier, more modest, Federal-style homes gave way to impressive residences built for its new affluent residents.

That year, two grand brick town houses were begun at Nos. 14 and 16. Completed a year later, No. 16 was purchased by Lanier. As the Lanier family moved in, a new home was begun next door at No. 18. It would become the residence of the Winslows.

The Winslow mansion was completed in 1856, an exceptionally handsome Italianate-style residence that rose four floors above an English basement. The architect distinguished the structure with a basement and parlor level base of brownstone that supported the brick upper stories.

The most striking feature was the parlor level with its three openings. Two floor-to-ceiling windows shared identical proportions with the entranceway—creating an unusual symmetry and appeal. Rather surprisingly, instead of the expected Italianate scrolled brackets below the cornice, the architect reverted to the more outdated dentiled cornice and fascia found on Greek Revival homes.

Nearly a century and a half later, the *AIA Guide to New York City* would dub the mansion "serene."

The Winslows lived in the house for only three years. In 1859, Dr. George H. Humphreys and his wife, May, purchased it. As had been the case with the Winslows, the deed was put in the wife's name, a common practice to ensure the financial stability of the widow should the income-earner die.

Although the Humphreys held on to the property until 1880, it appears they rented it for at least one year. In 1879 George and Harriet Hammond were living here when their son was born in the house on November 6.

The house was especially striking, even among its high-end neighbors.

The following year, the Humphreys sold the house to John E. Devlin. The importer was president of John E. Devlin & Co. and a director of the Houston, West Street and Pavonia Ferry Company; and of the Guardian Fire Insurance Company. Devlin sold the house in the fashionable neighborhood just three years later, in 1883, to wealthy sugar merchant Moses Lazarus, a member of the firm Johnson & Lazarus. Lazarus had retired in 1865 with what the *New York Times* deemed "a very large fortune." Now 67 years old, he was not in good health.

Lazarus's daughter, Emma, an established poet, was no doubt pleased with the location. The block had filled with artists. Two doors away lived painter John La Farge, and at No. 51 was the renowned Tenth Street Studio Building, where artists like Albert Bierstadt, Winslow Homer, and William Merritt Chase worked.

Emma sailed for Europe just weeks after the family moved in. At the time, Richard Morris Hunt's pedestal for the Statue of Liberty was already half completed, and in Paris the statue was ready to ship. All that was needed now was the raising of the money necessary to erect it.

In May, while Emma was still abroad, J. Carroll Beckwith and William Merritt Chase, both instructors at the Art Students League, agreed to organize a fund-raising art exhibition for the statue. In conjunction, writer Constance Cary Harrison asked two poets—one of them Emma Lazarus—to pen short verses for its opening.

Harrison would later recall, "I begged Miss Lazarus to give me some verses appropriate to the occasion. She was at first inclined to rebel against writing anything 'To order' as it were." Nevertheless, she completed "The New Colossus," a sonnet to "Liberty Enlightening the World" in time for the exhibition's opening on December 3, 1883. After that night, Emma Lazarus's stirring poem was largely forgotten.

On March 9, 1885, Moses Lazarus died in the house on West 10th Street from "a complication of diseases," according to the *Times*. The esteemed Jewish businessman had obtained memberships in some of the most exclusive clubs in town, a highly unusual achievement at the time.

That year, Emma set off on her second visit to Europe. When she returned to New York in September 1887, she was seriously ill. On November 20 the *Sun* reported, "Miss Emma Lazarus, the well-known poet, translator, and general writer for the magazines, died yesterday at 18 West Tenth Street, in this city, which was the home of her parents who are both dead."

Emma Lazarus was 36 years old. Newspapers reported that she "had been ill for about a year, though death was due to a recent development of congestion of the lungs." However, it is now believed that she probably died of Hodgkin's lymphoma. The funeral took place in the house the following morning.

The *Sun* noted, "Miss Lazarus was one of the leading woman writers of the age, a great and strong writer, and despite the fact that death came to her just as she had reached her prime, she had gained a place and made a mark in literature far above the achievements of many eminent lives well rounded by age."

Ironically, Lazarus's longest-lasting achievement would be her overlooked sonnet, "The New Colossus." When the Statue of Liberty was opened the year after her death, the poem played no part in the ceremony. Not until 1903, when the text was mounted in bronze on the pedestal, would the poem become linked with the monument.

The statue, intended as an embodiment of personal freedom and democracy, was transformed by Emma Lazarus's poem to a symbol of immigration and welcome.

The Lazarus family sold the house in May 1889 to stockbroker Henry B. Livingston, a member of one of New York's oldest and most respected families. Livingston was a partner in the firm of Lee, Livingston & Co., a member of the New York Stock Exchange. Like Moses Lazarus, he belonged to the Knickerbocker and Union Clubs.

The Livingston house was the scene of expected social entertainments. On December 7, 1895, the *New York Times* reported that, "Among the social incidents to-day will be [a reception by] Mrs. Henry R. Livingston, 18 West Tenth Street." That event was a tea given for Angelica Livingston, who was making her debut, and it was deemed by the newspaper to be one "of the largest" of the season.

In 1900 the Livingstons leased the house to banker Edwin M. Post, a member of the firm Thomas & Post. Born in Cincinnati, the wealthy financier was also president and director of the Express Coal Line and Georgia Car Co., vice-president and director of the Southern Iron Car Line, and secretary-treasurer and director of the Manhattan Car Trust Co., among other positions.

Post was in the house only a year, and in 1901, Mrs. Charles Lea rented it. The widowed Mrs. Lea used the mansion not only for meetings of her favorite social group, the Junior Thursday Evening Club, but also for debutante events for daughter Marjorie that year.

On January 11, Angelica Schuyler Church gave a luncheon "of twelve covers" in Marjorie's honor. It was quickly followed by two coming-out receptions in the 10th Street house, the second being held on January 25.

On March 21 the Junior Thursday Evening Club had a symposium in the house "where several members of the Comedy Club gave a little play," reported the *New York Times* the following day.

Mrs. Lea and her daughter moved on when, in August of that year, Henry B. Livingston sold the house to John Barry Ryan and his wife, Nina. Ryan was the son of the immensely wealthy Thomas Fortune Ryan, a prominent financier.

John Ryan had grown up in the family mansion at the northwest corner of Fifth Avenue and 12th Street. His mother, the former Ida M. Barry of Baltimore, died on October 17, 1917, and, much to the surprise and shock of the family, his father married Mrs. Cornelius C. Cuyler, "a prominent society woman of New York," according to the *Times*, just twelve days later.

The newspaper said, "John Barry Ryan, who lives at 18 West Tenth Street, would make no comment on his father's marriage." It added, "As far as could be learned last night, none of their families or friends even knew that they contemplated marriage."

The Ryans would rear four sons and a daughter in the house, not all of who would bring welcomed publicity to the family. John Barry Ryan's personal fortune was greatly increased upon the death of his father on November 23, 1928. Thomas Fortune Ryan left an estate of over $200 million, about one-fifth of which went to John.

That same year daughter Adele met nightclub entertainer Robert Johnston and his wife in Cap d'Antibes, France. There was an immediate attraction and when the Johnstons traveled to London the following winter, Adele decided to visit her sister there. Johnston was entertaining at the Night Life Club, of which the Prince of Wales was a member.

Adele visited the Johnstons during the day at their Pall Mall house and would come to the club in the evenings. The constant attention got on the nerves of the entertainer's wife, who complained that Adele wrote frequently to her husband and "willfully" tried to break up their marriage by sending him gifts.

When the Johnstons returned to their New York home nearby at 41 West 11th Street, Adele continued her pursuit of Johnston and "induced Mr. Johnston to accompany her on trips to Boston and on Oct. 3 [1929] persuaded him to escort her to the Park Chambers Hotel… and to register with her as 'Robert Johnston and wife,'" as reported in the *New York Times.*

Johnston left his wife and moved into the house next door to the Ryans, at No. 16 West 10th. The family's name was scandalously in the headlines when Muriel Johnston filed a $500,000 suit "for the loss of her husband's affections."

In June that same year, Adele's brother, Thomas Fortune Ryan II, was arrested in France as he prepared to sail to New York. He was charged with issuing checks for $2,600 without having the funds to back them. Then he upset the family further by marrying a divorcée, Mrs. Margaret Moorhead Rea. The marriage was kept generally quiet, but young Ryan displayed an uncanny ability to appear in the newspapers.

In March 1930 he drove his automobile into a truck, resulting in a slight skull fracture. Seven months later, in October, he obtained a divorce "on the ground of desertion." On June 27, 1931, the 32-year-old was in love again and secretly married the 23-year-old divorcée Mrs. Mayme Cook Masters.

John Barry Ryan had had his fill. On August 12 the *New York Times* reported that "News of the ceremony leaked out and rumors had been current since that Ryan's parents planned to have the marriage annulled."

The newspaper said on August 11, "Forced to choose… between his father's millions and his bride of six weeks, Thomas Fortune Ryan II today declared that he had refused to give up his wife and therefore had been disinherited by his father, John Barry Ryan of New York."

In the meantime, perhaps to ensure the quality of the block around his residence, John Barry Ryan purchased the three adjoining houses at Nos. 18, 20, and 22 that year.

Before long, it would be John Barry Ryan rather than his children who were bringing unwanted publicity to West 10th Street. The Ryans left the house in 1930, apparently in an effort to evade warrant servers and collection agents.

In 1932, Ryan was accused of "hiding or evading service of a suit in the Plaza Hotel" and by April 1933 his property was being seized to satisfy judgments against him.

Amazingly, the man who had inherited millions was now skirting servers. Two of his automobiles had been seized and on April 23 the *Times* reported that "representatives of Milton Eisenberg, attorney for W. Rossiter Redmond, who was appointed receiver for Mr. Ryan's property on Thursday, failed in their second attempt to station custodians in the Ryan home at 18 West Tenth Street here, where there are paintings and objects of art valued at about $1,000,000."

Indeed Ryan had filled the house (which was sitting unoccupied and guarded by the Holmes Electric Protective Company) with an impressive collection, including busts by Houdon. His financial problems plagued him for years to come. The government filed an income tax lien against him for $210,916.74 in 1937 and another in 1938.

John Barry Ryan died in 1942 and three years later Nina sold the house. In reporting the sale the *New York Times* said, "This is one of the picturesque old brick dwellings for which that neighborhood long was known, and is one of the few remaining in its original appearance, without remodeling. It dates back about a century." The newspaper noted, "It was acquired by the Ryan family in 1901 and occupied as their home until 1930, but has been vacant since then."

The amazingly unaltered house was purchased by attorney Charles Abrams, the visionary urban planner and housing expert who created the New York Housing Authority and was perhaps the first to use the expression "Socialism for the rich and capitalism for the poor."

At some point the carved moldings framing the upper-story windows were shaved flat, but no other significant changes were made to the house. While Charles worked on housing projects, his wife, artist Ruth Abrams, pursued her own career. She was Art Director at the Research Association of The New School between 1965 and 1966.

Charles died of cancer here in 1970. Ruth lived in the house until her death in March 1986, after which a *New York Times* critic called her "a woman unfairly neglected in a macho era."

In 1996 the basement was converted to a separate apartment; however, today the upper floors remain a single-family house. The 28-foot-wide residence is an elegant remnant of old West 10th Street, as well as where one of America's most moving poems was penned.

ASCH BUILDING

23–29 WASHINGTON PLACE

Early on the morning of Saturday, March 25, 1911, Mary Herman pulled on her coat, shut the door behind her, and started off to work at the Triangle Waist Factory near Washington Square.

The building to which Mary headed was the Asch Building, completed in January 1901. Built by furrier Joseph J. Asch with Ole Olsen, it was intended to be the latest in fireproof design, with an iron and steel framework clad in non-combustible terra-cotta. Because it stood only 135 feet high, fire laws allowed wooden floors and window frames. Although sprinklers were not required by law, the initial plans did include a fire alarm system, fire hoses on all floors, two staircases per floor, and an iron fire escape clinging to the exterior wall of the light court.

Further fire precautions were added by the Buildings Department, which called for an additional set of fire stairs and directed that the rear fire escape "must lead to something more substantial than a skylight."

The architect, John Woolley, however, argued against the additional staircase. Because the floors were all open, being loft manufacturing spaces, and the planned stairs were far from each other, he reasoned that the exterior fire escape counted as a third staircase. The Building Department accepted his argument.

The finished loft building was attractive in ecru-colored brick and terra-cotta. Designed in the latest Renaissance Revival style, it was embellished with ornate terra-cotta panels and wreaths. The 10th floor stood out with a series of arched windows lining up beneath a deeply overhanging cornice.

The Triangle Waist Company—often referred to as the Triangle Shirtwaist Company—set up its factory in the top three floors of the Asch Building at Nos. 23–29 Washington Place. Here, aside from the offices on the 10th floor, young women mostly in their teens and early 20s bent their backs over sewing machines constructing shirtwaist blouses—the high-necked, tailored garments that were the height of fashion.

The girls were poorly paid, conditions were miserable, and work was hard. When the International Ladies Garment Workers Union struck in 1909, Triangle retaliated by firing 150 sympathizers. From that point on, owners Max Blanck and

Isaac Harris locked the girls in, kept the light court windows shuttered and ruled the sewing floor by fear. Sewing girls told of raising their eyes from their machines only when they were certain they would not be caught. Speaking was forbidden and restroom breaks were closely monitored. The women were all searched upon leaving the building at quitting time. Anyone wishing to work for Blanck and Harris was required to provide her own needles and thread.

Mary Herman was working on the 9th floor that Saturday. The girls would all be going home in ten minutes—at 4:45 p.m. There was unspoken relief in the room.

Meanwhile, downstairs on the 8th floor a pile of fabric somehow caught

On March 25, 1911 fire fighters battle the flames as the building is engulfed.

fire on a table. Paper patterns hanging above quickly ignited and the blaze grew. When a floor manager rushed to the fire hose in the hall, the rotted hose crumbled. The bookkeeper, Mary Loventhal, called the offices on the top floor and warned of the fire. In the frenzy, no one thought to notify the 9th floor, where Mary Herman was working.

Most of the panicked women on the 8th floor rushed to the elevator and stairs and escaped; however, others, unable to make it to the stairs or wedge into the crowded elevators, jumped to their deaths.

With the bookkeeper's alarm from the 8th floor, those on the top floor dashed to the stairways and all but one survived.

Meanwhile, on the 9th floor business went on as usual. When the closing bell clanged, the girls accepted their pay envelopes and headed for the coatroom. Suddenly, the fire reached the floor. As the room filled with smoke, panicked girls fell over tables and machinery. As workers crammed into the stairways, a barrel of machine oil near one set of stairs suddenly exploded, blocking that exit. Mary Herman was seen rushing to a door, which, to her terror, was locked.

Lillian Wilner fought with the iron shutters on a light court window, finally prying them open, and desperate women packed onto the 17-inch-wide iron fire escape. To their utter dismay the drop ladder at the bottom had never been installed and they were trapped on the metal escape.

Emergency workers examine heaped bodies on the pavement.

As more and more women crammed onto the fire escape, their combined weight and the heat of the fire caused it to collapse. The workers plunged to the pavement of the light court.

As other women were jammed into the slowly descending elevators, workers jumped into the elevator shafts, landing on top of the cabs. Others tried to slide down the elevator cables.

The Fire Department arrived but, according to the *New York Times*, the fire engines had difficulty getting near the building due to the number of bodies scattered about the sidewalk and street. "While more bodies crashed down among them they worked with desperation to run their ladders into position and spread their fire nets," reported the newspaper.

Life nets broke apart with the force of bodies falling from the upper stories and when the fire ladders were extended, they were too short to reach the floors where victims were trapped. Police Captain Dominick Henry recalled "a scene I hope I never see again. Dozens of girls were hanging from the ledges. Others, their dresses on fire, were leaping from the windows."

It was all over within 30 minutes. Mary Herman never went home that evening. Neither did 145 other shirtwaist workers. A wave of horror accompanied the story as it swept across the nation, fostering the beginnings of strengthened fire codes, better work conditions, and stronger labor unions.

The Asch (Brown) Building as it appears today. Scores of young women flung themselves from the cornice under the arched windows of the 10th floor.

Days later, most of the bodies, burned or disfigured beyond recognition, were still unidentified. Finally on March 31, Mayor William Jay Gaynor decided that the city would bury the final fourteen unidentified victims in a lot in Evergreen Cemetery in East New York. Five days later, over 80,000 mourners filed up Fifth Avenue in a procession sponsored by the Women's Trade Union League and Local 25 for the unknown victims. Hundreds of thousands of workers walked away from their jobs that afternoon to view the procession.

Blanck and Harris were indicted for manslaughter in the death of Mary Herman on April 11 for locking the factory door in violation of New York State labor laws. The jury, however, found that proving the owners knew about the locked door was impossible, and the pair was acquitted. Blanck and Harris received $200,000 from their insurance claim for fire damages. Twenty-three families each received a $75 settlement from Joseph J. Asch for the lost lives.

Despite the overwhelming tragedy and loss of life, the Asch Building was actually little damaged. The terra-cotta cladding and iron and steel framework withstood the heat and flames as the designer intended. Joseph Asch hired architects Maynicke & Franke to correct logistical defects. Their work included adding a new fire escape, removing the iron shutters, and constructing two large water tanks on the roof. In 1912 a modern sprinkler system was installed. After the restoration and renovations it was renamed the Greenwich Building and continued its use as a manufacturing loft.

New York University rented the 8th floor, where the fire had started, in 1915. A year later plans were announced to install a library and classrooms here. In 1918 the school took over the 9th floor and a year later expanded to the 10th—now inhabiting the three floors formerly home to the Triangle Waist Company.

By the 1920s the university had taken over the entire building. German-born philanthropist Frederick Brown purchased the structure and, on February 28, 1929, signed it over to New York University. The school renamed the building the Brown Building.

Every year, on March 25, firefighters, city officials, union leaders, and fashion industry employees hold a ceremony at the Brown Building to commemorate the tragedy of March 25, 1911. A fire ladder is hoisted to the 6th floor—the extent that the ladders reached that day, too short to help those dying above—and a fire bell tolls once for each of the 146 lives lost.

VILLAGE CIGARS AND THE MYSTERY MOSAIC

CHRISTOPHER STREET AND SEVENTH AVENUE

While the neighborhood changes, the Village Cigars store has been an unaltered presence at the sharp point where Christopher Street runs into Seventh Avenue for nearly a century. Slathered with metal signs and often peeling paint, the eccentric little building never seems to change.

But more interesting than the building is the mysterious little triangular mosaic imbedded into the pavement just in front of the cigar store's entrance. It is all that remains of the David and Goliath–type struggle of a man who fought City Hall. And won.

At the turn of the 20th century, Seventh Avenue terminated at 11th Street in Greenwich Village as originally laid out in the 1811 Commissioners' Plan. The famous midtown grid pattern of streets and avenues was designed by a committee of three in an astonishing example of urban preplanning—decades before the city would expand that far north.

In 1911, however, exactly a century later, civic groups pushed to extend Seventh Avenue south to better connect midtown to downtown as well as to augment the commercial access to the Village. The extension would also allow for construction of the IRT subway along Seventh Avenue southward.

Armed with the power of eminent domain, the City seized property in the path of the projected avenue and, like Sherman cutting through Georgia, demolished everything in its way, including historic buildings like the 1840 Greek Revival Bedford Street Methodist Church and the not-so-historic Voorhis Apartments.

And that's when the fight began.

The Voorhis was a five-story apartment building facing Christopher Street and owned by David Hess. Hess fought the City in an attempt to save his building, but lost. All that was left of his property in 1914 was a tiny triangle of land of approximately 500 square inches.

The City, in an act of what Hess must have considered the ultimate insult, requested him to donate the little plot to New York to become part of the public

The entrance to the little store is in the chamfered point—cut off because David Hess owned the triangle.

sidewalk. Hess refused. The City had taken his building but they could not have his triangle.

David Hess went to court against the City of New York and won. When the little Village Cigars store went up a few years later, Hess commissioned the in-your-face mosaic. Everyone who stood on that corner would know that David Hess still owned the few inches of pavement.

In 1938, having made their point, the Hess Estate sold the tiny triangle to United-Cigar Whelan Stores, the chain that owned Village Cigars, for $1,000—about $2 per inch. Today, Village Cigars looks exactly as it does in any vintage photograph. Its sole architectural feature is the interesting pressed and painted metal cornice. While not a significant building, it remains an old friend in the Village. And the story of the little mosaic triangle in front of it is priceless.

David Hess made sure that his victory against the City would be documented for posterity.

LOWER EAST SIDE AND EAST VILLAGE

GENERAL SLOCUM
MEMORIAL FOUNTAIN

235 EAST 22ND STREET

BREESE
CARRIAGE HOUSE
150 E. 22ND STREET.

BREESE CARRIAGE HOUSE

150 EAST 22ND STREET

The wealthy Breese family traced its roots in America to English-born Sidney Breese, who died in 1767 and was buried in Trinity Churchyard. Eloise Lawrence Breese could count among her ancestors Judge Breese, who served in the Continental Army. Her mother, the former Mary Louise Parsons, was a cousin of Hamilton Fish.

Eloise inherited her mother's unconventional independence. In 1893 the *New York Times* noted that only two women "in this part of the country" were eligible as yacht owners. One of them was Mrs. William L. Breese "who owns the sloop *Eloise*."

The Breese family lived in a wide, comfortable home at 35 East 22nd Street in the fashionable Madison Square neighborhood. Next door at No. 33 lived Mrs. Elizabeth B. Grannis, a self-appointed combatant against sin. Mrs. Grannis was president of the National Christian League for the Promotion of Purity. In December 1894 her search for sin would place her squarely in the social territory of Eloise Breese.

The unmarried Eloise—she preferred that the press refer to her as Miss E. L. Breese—took her own box at the Metropolitan Opera House. Her Grand Tier box, number 43, was near those of Isaac Fletcher, Joseph Pulitzer, and Charles Gould. Women's evening fashions in the 1890s included elegant off-the-shoulder evening gowns with plunging necklines. Known as décolletage, the French fashion was shocking to some Victorian minds.

The *Evening World* reported on December 1, 1894, that Mrs. Grannis lately "has been engaged in seeing for herself just how wicked New York really is." Having visited (escorted by her brother, Dr. Bartlett) "nearly all the dance and concert halls, theatres, joints, missions and dives in this city," she turned her focus to the Metropolitan Opera and its wealthy patrons.

Mrs. Grannis took an *Evening World* reporter in tow and explained the Purity League's plans to abolish the décolleté dress. "What we want to do is to call public attention to the evil, and by this means to shame people into dressing differently."

She admitted, when the reporter said that judging from the Metropolitan audience, "Mrs. Grannis's idea cannot be said to have borne much fruit," that it would take time. She blamed the absence of social purity on two forces. "One reason is the décolleté dress; the other and greater is the round dance."

Mrs. Grannis approved of "a modest square dance like the lanciers or the minuet," but waltzing "and every other form of round dance is, per se, sinful."

The equally strong-minded Eloise Breese disagreed. And the two women would make their differences known repeatedly. While the social reformer railed against the high fashion of the young socialite and her wealthy friends, Eloise frequently complained to authorities about "smells" coming from the Grannis home.

Following her father's death and her mother's remarriage and move to England, the independent Eloise was a marked feature among New York society. In 1901 she commissioned Sidney V. Stratton to design a private carriage house at No. 150 East 22nd Street, a few blocks to the east of her home. Private stables were as much a reflection of one's social status as one's home and carriages, and Eloise's would not disappoint. Stratton designed it in the Flemish Revival style that had been popular, especially on the Upper West Side, for over a decade.

The style reflected New York's Dutch beginnings and the Breese structure featured the expected stepped gable. Stratton placed the two-story structure on a limestone base and trimmed the warm Roman brick with limestone. A spreading peacock tail of oversized voussoirs highlighted the double carriage doors and the three upper openings visually became one by the introduction of an encompassing, limestone trimmed blind arch.

Like her mother, Eloise sailed her own yacht. The *Elsa* flew the burgee of the New York Yacht Club—a highly unusual accomplishment for a woman at the time. Although Eloise summered mostly in Tuxedo, where she maintained a sprawling mansion, the *Elsa* was often found moored below the cliffs of Newport. Captain C. M. Toren skippered the craft for years.

As Eloise's carriage house was being completed, she sailed the *Elsa* to Newport to participate in the July 30, 1901, harbor fete in honor of the North Atlantic squadron. Admiral Higginson's fleet was assembled in the harbor and a full day of activities—including an exhibition of the submarine torpedo boat *Holland*—was planned.

The *New-York Tribune* noted the following day that "the principal event was the illumination in the evening.... The most picturesque sight was in the harbor, where the illuminations were on a most gorgeous scale." The yachts were all lit "brilliantly" and the newspaper pointed out that the *Elsa* was one of "the most attractive ones."

In 1902, Eloise L. Breese had had enough of her pious next-door neighbor, and she purchased the Grannis house "with the understanding that it was to be pulled down," said the *Sun*. But she had second thoughts and once the social reformer had moved out "the temple of social reform and universal peace has been turned into a boarding house," the newspaper reported later.

The rooms where Mrs. Grannis had held meetings of other virtuous women and church leaders were now decorated by Eloise "in the highest form of boarding-house art with bows and arrows of primitive peoples and the heads of savages in war paint."

But she wasn't done yet.

In May 1903, Eloise sued Elizabeth Grannis for $249 saying that "when she moved out, [she] took with her a bathtub and the chandeliers."

Mrs. Grannis appeared baffled and unruffled. "How silly," she told reporters. "Think of going to court for just one little bathtub. It is my personal, individual tub. Of course I took it with me. I told them I was going to, but offered to sell it to them with the chandeliers."

The reformer complained that the Breese family had always been a problem. "What a flibberty-gibberty commotion it is. I lived beside the Breeses eighteen years and never met them, but they were forever sending in to complain of smells they thought they smelled and to see if there wasn't a fire or a leak or something in my house."

The feud between the former neighbors would eventually die away. In November 1906, Eloise married Adam Norrie. Upon her death on January 28, 1921, she added significantly to the collection of the Metropolitan Museum of Art by bequeathing two important paintings, one by Rousseau and another by Corot (*The Wheelwright's Yard on the Bank of the Seine*). Even more important, she left the museum the incomparable seventeenth-century Audenarde tapestries representing the history of the Sabines.

The Breese carriage house, no longer needed by Eloise after her marriage, was converted almost immediately into the headquarters of the New York Association for the Improvement of the Poor. It underwent another renovation in 1923 when it became a bakery.

A decade later, with horses having been replaced by motorcars, the building was once again converted. Still owned by the Breese Estate, it now had an apartment on the upper floor and "storage for four cars" at ground level. In February 1935 Raymond C. Phillips leased what the *Times* called "the modern two-story garage" from the estate.

In the mid-1940s retired police officer Thomas A. Smith lived upstairs. On July 24, 1948, the 63-year-old was driving along East 25th Street when a 7-year-old girl, Gloria Maracamo, darted into the path of his car. The driver was so upset that thirty minutes later, as he tried to tell police what had happened, he collapsed with a fatal heart attack.

Only the façade of
Eloise Breese's carriage
house remains.

By the second half of the twentieth century the carriage houses along the block
had been demolished for apartment buildings—except for Eloise Breese's. In 1965
the anachronistic little building was being used as an "architect's fine arts studio
and office" along with parking for two cars on the ground floor, and a one-family
apartment above, according to Department of Buildings records.

Then in 2006 change came to No. 150 East 22nd Street. The rear wall was
shaved off and a modern, glass-walled residence constructed behind. The
5,200-square-foot, single-family house preserved the façade of the Breese stable,
but at a significant cost. The *AIA Guide to New York City* called it a "nice deal for the
developer's bank accounts; lousy deal for landmarks preservation."

GENERAL SLOCUM
MEMORIAL FOUNTAIN

TOMPKINS SQUARE PARK

Gradually tragedy fades from our historic memory. Little by little grievous disasters become, at best, stories protracted by bronze plaques or statues; at worst, totally forgotten. Hundreds of people pass the beautifully veined pink marble fountain in Tompkins Square every day. Hardly anyone knows why it is there.

At the turn of the last century, the Lower East Side was populated by German immigrants, earning the district the name *Kleindeutschland* or "Little Germany." On the morning of Wednesday, June 15, 1904, the members of St. Mark's Evangelical Lutheran Church at 323 East 6th Street near Second Avenue set off on their 17th annual summer outing. For $350, they had chartered a 235-foot steam sidewheeler, the *General Slocum* for a day trip up the East River, across the Long Island Sound to a picnic grove on Long Island.

They never made it there.

Because it was a Wednesday morning (the men were at work), the boat was filled mostly with women and children. Over 1,300 passengers boarded the steamer, which carried a crew of thirty-five. The church party was unaware of the *General Slocum*'s recent history of problems—running aground several times and, at least twice, colliding with another ship. Worse yet, Captain William Van Schaick had never practiced fire drills with his crew, as required by law. Life preservers and fire hoses had not been inspected since the craft was constructed thirteen years earlier.

The ship pushed off from the Third Street Pier at 9:30 a.m. A band on board played carefree tunes and children ran about on the upper decks. By 10:00 it was entering the treacherous Hells Gate section of the river. It was at this point that onlookers on shore, hearing the music, noticed smoke billowing from below decks and began wildly gesturing to those on board.

The fire below decks intensified when it reached a paint locker filled with gasoline and other flammable liquids. Panicked passengers rushed for life jackets, most

Scores of passengers line the pier waiting to board the
General Slocum for an earlier outing.

of which fell apart in their hands—the canvas fabric having rotted after years of
exposure to the elements. The cork filling in the rest of the vests had granulated
over time, so when mothers laced their children into the vests and tossed them
overboard, they watched in horror as the cork absorbed the water and pulled their
children under.

Captain Van Schaick told the *New York Times* the following day that he looked out
from his pilothouse and saw "a fierce blaze—the wildest I have ever seen."

Crew members tried in vain to fight the conflagration with rotten fire hoses that
burst under the water pressure. Having been repeatedly painted in place, lifeboats
were stuck to the ship's side. Pandemonium reigned as children jumped into the
river, some sucked under in the turbulent Hell Gate eddies, others pulled into the
side wheels and beaten to death. Women who jumped overboard in their woolen
Edwardian garments were quickly weighed down and drowned.

The captain steered the ship towards North Brother Island in the Bronx, into the
wind, which fanned the flames and intensified the conflagration. Suddenly, the main
deck collapsed, dropping hundreds of women and children into the inferno below.

As was the case with the "Miracle on the Hudson"—the US Airways jetliner
that landed in the river a century later—New Yorkers rushed to the rescue. Two
fireboats, at least a dozen tugboats, ferries, a police boat—over 100 vessels in all—
hurried to the scene. For most it was too late. Within a span of fifteen minutes
the *General Slocum* was burned to the waterline. Only 321 of the 1,300 people on
board survived; the rest perished either by fire or drowning. It was the greatest loss
of life in New York City until September 11, 2001. The *New York Times* reported,

By the time rescuers arrived, the *General Slocum* had burned to the water line.

"The disaster stands unparalleled among those of its kind. Whole families have been wiped out. In many instances a father is left to grieve alone for wife and children, and there was hardly a home in the parish, whence but a few hours before a laughing happy crowd went on its holiday, that was not in deep mourning last night."

The entire nation was stunned. Little Germany was decimated and would never recover. Most of those who survived moved away.

The Sympathy Society of German Ladies commissioned sculptor Bruno Louis Zimm to design a memorial fountain to those lost. Dedicated in 1906, his 9-foot-high stele is sculpted of pink Tennessee marble. On the front, above the carved lion's head spout and basin, a low-relief sculpture depicts two innocent children staring off towards the sea.

The inscription reads, "They were Earth's purest children, young and fair."

The Sympathy Society of German Ladies installed the fountain so that the unspeakable loss of lives on the *General Slocum* would never be forgotten. We have, unfortunately, forgotten.

The tranquil and poignant bas relief depicts two children gazing off toward the sea.

THE SCENE OF
THE PERFECT CRIME

235 EAST 22ND STREET

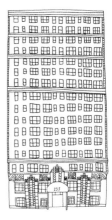

As the Great Depression darkened the country, American moviegoers escaped into glamorous Manhattan penthouses and Park Avenue apartments via the silver screen. As Ginger Rogers and Ruby Keeler, in clinging satin evening dresses, entered sunken living rooms with sleek Art Deco furnishings, the worries over rent payments and the reality of the bread lines outside were briefly forgotten.

Just months after the Stock Market crash, architect brothers Edward and George Blum started work on a massive Art Deco apartment building at the northwest corner of 22nd Street and Second Avenue. Completed in 1931, it may not have sat on Park Avenue, but it was definitely Fred Astaire-ready.

The building was marketed to the financially comfortable, and potential residents were shown apartments surrounding an interior garden courtyard, with hand-painted bathroom tiles, parquet floors, and stylish tray ceilings.

As the sixteen-story building was nearing completion on February 1, 1931, the *New York Times* commented on its features. "The façade of the new house will be of polychrome terra-cotta and marble and brown brick. Apartments will range from one to four rooms and many will have terraces. There will also be five- and seven-room penthouse suites. Special features include wood-burning fireplaces, tile showers, dressing rooms, incinerators and mail chute."

The Blums tossed aside the gloom and doom of the Depression and wrapped the new building with a colorful band of terra-cotta. Here, pointy zigzags like mountain ranges sat above a gentle wave pattern like a river. The southwestern color scheme—turquoise, green, ochre, and navy—prompted one architectural historian to call it "Pueblo Deco." The Art Deco design culminated in the two-story entrance with its three stylized terra-cotta waterfalls.

Depression or not, the building filled with tenants. Robert E. Hill took one of the terraced suites immediately upon the building's opening. Agnes C. Tufverson, a professional woman whom the *New York Times* called "a brilliant corporation lawyer," moved in. The unmarried attorney's maid did not live in the building, but arrived in the mornings.

Ludwig Schopp moved in on September 1, 1933. He hung paintings and etchings on the walls valued at $10,000. Although the 38-year-old held a PhD from the University of Bonn, the economy, perhaps, forced him to earn a living as an insurance salesman.

The economy also forced Schopp to skim money from his premium collections—a lot of money. To make up the shortage, he devised a plan to collect the insurance on his art collection: He would set his apartment on fire.

Schopp promised Dorothy L. Tipping that he would pay her $1,000 of the insurance proceeds if she would set the fire. On Monday night, November 29, he made himself conspicuously not at home. In the meantime, Dorothy

The architects used bold, colorful terra cotta and creative brickwork to create an Art Deco beauty.

Tipping entered the apartment, piled the etchings and paintings in the middle of the living room floor, and then set fire to the couch and the bed.

Fire investigators, understandably, found the fire to be suspicious. The investigation of Assistant Fire Marshal Isidore Srebnick quickly tracked down Schopp, who was hiding out in the apartment of Otto Stemman at No. 37-40 81st Street in Jackson Heights, Queens. When the marshal arrived at the apartment with a team of detectives, "Schopp ran into another room. As the detectives followed, Schopp pushed himself through a window and was captured as he attempted to jump to the street nearly forty feet below," reported the *Times.*

Both Schopp and his female accomplice confessed.

In the meantime, Agnes Tufverson was doing well for herself. She was working in the law firm of Myron C. Herrick and was making an enviable income. Two months before the soon-to-be arsonist Schopp moved into her building, the 43-year-old Tufverson was in Europe on vacation. In July, while on a "boat-train" between London and Southampton, a handsome Yugoslavian Army captain struck up a conversation.

The middle-aged spinster was soon hooked. Ivan Poderjay was at least ten years younger than Agnes. The *New York Times* said he was "handsome and described as 'a very charming personality.'" He told Agnes that he was on his way to the United States to sell a patent to an American company for a door lock that would reap him a million dollars.

What Agnes Tufverson did not know was that just a month earlier, on May 12, 1934, the British magazine *John Bull* had published an article about the smooth-talker sitting next to her. It told how he had conned two older women out of their life savings.

As fate would have it, the pair traveled to New York on the same steamer from Southampton and Agnes was swept off her feet. Before the ship docked, they had decided to marry. After Poderjay returned to England for a short visit, the couple was married in the Little Church Around the Corner—the wedding church—on December 4.

The newlyweds moved into Agnes's apartment on East 22nd Street and booked passage on the *S.S. Hamburg,* leaving on December 20, for their extended European honeymoon. Agnes had her personal shopper, Susan Sawtell, purchase over $1,000 worth of lingerie and gowns for her trousseau. On the day of the voyage, Agnes's maid, Eva, helped the couple pack. Agnes made a telephone call to her sisters in Detroit, saying goodbye and telling them she would return by April.

While Eva and Agnes packed, Poderjay walked to a local pharmacy and purchased ten dollars worth of razor blades—enough at Depression Era prices to shave an entire Army base. He also asked the elevator operator where he could purchase "a large trunk" in the neighborhood.

The couple took a cab to the pier at 46th Street and the Hudson River with their luggage; they then returned to the apartment without the trunks between 10 and 11:00 p.m. Eva was still there cleaning up. She later reported that Agnes was agitated and that Poderjay was surly. Agnes sent her home and told her not to return the following day, but to come as usual the day after.

The elevator operators never saw Agnes leave the building after that. When Eva returned on December 22, she found Poderjay going through Agnes's personal papers. He told the maid, "She found it necessary to go to Philadelphia"; but he told the building staff that she had gone on to Europe ahead of him.

Eva was told to burn all of Agnes's personal papers and Poderjay left the apartment. He set sail on the White Star steamer *Olympic* with four trunks—including the new, exceptionally large one he had purchased—and six smaller bags. It was the last Eva or the staff at 235 East 22nd Street would see of Agnes Tufverson or Ivan Poderjay.

When Agnes's sisters had not heard from her four months later, their concerns launched an investigation. It was found that Agnes had withdrawn $17,000 in cash from several banks, that she had given her husband $5,000 in the form of a draft in London, and that all her stocks and securities were missing. It was also discovered that the army captain was an imposter, in no way affiliated with the military.

Stylized waterfalls flank the front door where Agnes Tufverson
entered with her new husband in 1934.

Also missing was the extra-large trunk that Poderjay had taken aboard the
Olympic. He was tracked down in Vienna and questioned by Viennese police. He told
them he had no idea where his wife was and that "she is probably on a world tour."
On June 20, 1934, the *New York Times* reported, "While bewildered authorities
here sought feverishly yesterday for some tangible clue to the whereabouts of
Agnes C. Tufverson, dead or alive, chemists in Vienna tried to analyze reddish
stains found on one of her wardrobe trunks in the apartment of Ivan Poderjay, her
Yugoslav husband."

In the days before advanced forensic techniques, the stains, although reported
by the Viennese newspaper the *Telegraf* to be bloodstains, were frustratingly vague.
"Preliminary microscopic examination failed to reveal the exact nature of the
stains," said the *Times*.

Further raising the eyebrows of authorities was the discovery that Poderjay had
married Marguerite Suzanne Ferrand in London on March 22, 1933, just four months
after his marriage to Agnes. When his newest bride was questioned, her attorney
claimed she was "just another victim of another clever swindler." Authorities were
concerned because in her possession were "certain garments that were at one time
the property of Miss Tufverson."

Assistant Chief Inspector John J. Sullivan of the New York Police Department
told reporters that, according to Cunard stewards, Poderjay had spent most of the
time on the voyage to Southampton in his stateroom. "It was an outside stateroom,"

Sullivan explained… It might even be possible that if he took the trunk with him that he might have disposed of it on his way across."

Agnes's sisters were alarmed by more evidence. The *Times* said they were "discouraged by the news that among the articles found in Poderjay's Vienna apartment was a brief case that Agnes Tufverson had prized as a good-luck symbol. She had carried it with her everywhere and would not have yielded it to anyone if she were alive."

In the meantime, Poderjay's new wife told investigators that Agnes "often threatened suicide, but I am sure she is alive and will come forward to clear him."

To the extreme frustration of Viennese and New York police, despite the highly incriminating circumstantial evidence, there was no body and not enough evidence to charge Poderjay with murder. He was extradited to New York in January 1935 on charges of bigamy and spent five years in Auburn Prison.

After his sentence (during which he lost an eye in a fight with another inmate) he was deported to Yugoslavia. Authorities shook their heads, fully believing that the con man had dismembered his wife and dropped her body parts overboard during his voyage to Southampton. He had committed the perfect crime.

The Art Deco beauty on East 22nd Street attracted little more scandal or drama in the succeeding years. As World War II erupted in Europe, esteemed artist Marjorie Schiele fled Europe and moved to New York. On November 1, 1940, she leased "a furnished suite" here. While living here, she became friends with other expatriate artists including Piet Mondrian, Marcel Duchamp, Lyonel Feininger, Max Ernst, and Fernand Lèger.

The striking apartment building that shrugged off the gloom of the Depression remains nearly unchanged after more than eighty years. The windows have been replaced as have the entrance doors, yet it is a striking example of Art Deco residential architecture in a somewhat surprising location.

UNION SQUARE

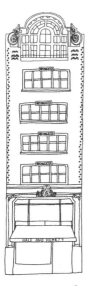

HOUGHTON-MIFFLIN BUILDING
11 EAST 17TH STREET

CENTURY ASSOCIATION BUILDING
109-111 EAST 15TH STREET

W AND J SLOANE
BUILDING
880-888 BROADWAY

The completed building was like nothing else along the block.

HOUGHTON, MIFFLIN & CO. BUILDING

11 EAST 17TH STREET

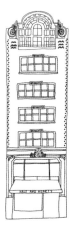

In 1880, when its senior members retired, the publishing firm of Hurd and Houghton reestablished itself as Houghton, Mifflin and Company. The company not only published scholarly works like law books and dictionaries, but also printed popular novels and magazines such as the *North American Review* and the *Riverside Magazine for Young People.* Just two years earlier it had purchased the *Atlantic Monthly.*

Shortly after the change in name and management the publisher moved its New York offices uptown from Astor Place to the Union Square neighborhood. The firm moved into the former Gross mansion, a pre-Civil War house at 11 East 17th Street. A generation earlier the block had been lined with high-end residences in keeping with its location between Fifth Avenue and Union Square. Now, as commerce encroached on the area, wealthy citizens moved northward and their homes were converted to businesses.

In 1899 in its "Catalogue of Authors Whose Works are published by Houghton Mifflin and Company" the firm described the sections of its four-story brick house. "They occupy a portion of a building which still discloses in the drawing-room, now filled with books and desks, the former use as a family residence. Two of the partners have their office here, and the various interests of the house are served, the department for the sale of standard libraries being especially active."

Houghton, Mifflin and Company established its retail store on the lower level. The upper floors remained residential and were rented out to boarders. Attorney William Cleveland Cox and his wife, the former actress Alice Gleason, lived here in 1888, and well-known actor Walden Ramsay died in the house on October 6, 1895.

Houghton, Mifflin's keen marketing was evident in its 1889 advertisement extolling the new paperback edition of *John Ward, Preacher.* The new release was described in the *New-York Tribune*: "Mrs. Deland's remarkable Novel, which has excited so great interest through the English-speaking world, is now issued in tasteful paper covers, at Fifty Cents. It is the first number of The Riverside Paper Series, of Standard and Popular Copyright Novels to be issued Semi-Monthly."

In December 1901, two decades after Houghton, Mifflin moved into the old mansion, the Gross family sold the property to Daniel B. Freedman. Three months later he resold it to "a Mr. Snyder" according to the *Sun*. The newspaper noted, "The buyer will either build a loft building or resell the property with a building loan."

Indeed, Snyder resold the building, this time to James A. Campbell, who turned it over yet again in October 1902 to "a Mr. Stillwell" for $60,000. That deal, apparently, fell through and in 1903, Campbell, with his partner William Clement, laid plans for a modern loft building to replace the old house.

Campbell & Clement razed the building and commissioned respected architects Israels & Harder to design an up-to-date store and loft building. The architects completed in 1904 a seven-story store and loft building, which made a strong statement among its neighbors.

Among the proper, expected commercial designs of the other structures going up along the block, Israels & Harder introduced an energetic splash of Art Nouveau. For Houghton, Mifflin and Company's bookstore, a two-story retail space soared from the sidewalk, framed in stone. Heavy moldings—picture frame-like—embraced the expansive windows and a carved medallion flanked by cornucopia announced the address.

Above, seven stories of brown-red brick engulfed centered, grouped windows, culminating in a double-height studio, sun-drenched by a massive Palladian-inspired window. Here an ambitious terra-cotta arch capped it all, flanked by wonderful, scrolled over-sized volutes.

With the modern building completed, Campbell had better luck in selling the property. In January 1904 it was sold, only to be re-sold to Inter-River Realty and Construction Company on February 6.

Houghton, Mifflin and Company moved into its new office and retail space, and the upper floors quickly filled with a variety of tenants. In 1905 Lemonoff, Saxe & Co., a skirt manufacturer, was busily making women's apparel here. Other clothing manufacturers included Snyder & Parnes, and cloak and suit makers Sigmund Katz.

Interestingly, Houghton, Mifflin and Company was not the only bookseller to take space in the building. Lemcke & Buechner dealt in art books and in 1906 offered the first folio in a series by Dr. Paul Herrmann of Dresden on "paintings of the ancients." The folio pictured the wall paintings surviving in Pompeii, Rome, Herculaneum, and Stabiae, along with Italian mosaics.

There were to be a total of sixty books in the series, each with ten plates. Six books would be published annually. The over-sized books were available by subscription only, and the *New York Times* noted that "subscriptions to less than twenty parts will not be accepted."

Another bookseller, Strauss & Muller, was in the building by 1910. Perhaps the concentrated competition was too much for Houghton, Mifflin; or perhaps they were simply "following the steady march of business uptown," as *Walden's Stationer and Printer* put it. Either way, the publisher left the building in 1911 for a new building near Grand Central Terminal.

No. 11 East 17th Street continued to be home to apparel manufacturers and small businesses throughout the century. Art Craft Fixture and Novelty Company was here in the 1920s, offering electrical lighting fixtures. Bricker & Ratchick, makers of "cloaks and suits" leased the seventh floor and added another full floor in 1931. A year earlier Isidore & Charles Levin, dealers in "notions," took the retail store and basement.

In the mid 1960s Amalgamated Union Local 15 had its offices here. The union was headed by Benjamin Ross, "sometimes known as 'Benny the Bug,'" according to the *New York Times* on December 20, 1964. The shady operations of the union caused John F. Funke of the National Labor Relations Board to describe it as "one that a government agency would not willingly endorse."

During a trial before the Board that month, attorney Nathan Goldman said that Ross "practiced his now well-recognized pattern of extortion, muscle and intimidation."

The 1960s and '70s were a time of political and social radicalism in America. The building became headquarters for the Underground Press Syndicate, a network of counterculture publications including the *East Village Other,* the *Berkeley Barb,* the *Paper*, and *Fifth Estate.*

The Syndicate held a news conference in the building on July 13, 1970, concerning a three-day rock festival to be held on Randall's Island. The *New York Times* listed organizations represented at the conference: the Young Lords, the White Panther Party, and the Revolutionary Youth Party Collective, "which represents such groups as the Gay Liberation Front, the Committee to Defend the New York Panther 21, the Youth International Party and the Underground Press Syndicate."

In 1998 the building was converted to apartments—one per floor. Early that year aspiring artist Kobo leased the astounding top floor with its vast 16-foot-tall window (his real name was Oded Kobo, but Tracie Rozhon of the *New York Times* explained "he hasn't used his first name since he was 3").

The artist enjoyed what the *Times* article described as "a two-story living room, tin ceilings and rare side windows." The 2,400-square-foot studio/apartment cost him $3,500 per month. Unfortunately for Kobo, his lease—which the landlords were not interested in renewing—was for a mere nine months.

Although the windows have been replaced and the lower two floors have been altered, the wonderful 1904 loft building remains a refreshing and unusual example of Art Nouveau architecture in Manhattan.

W. & J. SLOANE BUILDING

880–888 BROADWAY

The stretch of Broadway just above Union Square saw the rise of grand emporiums in the years after the Civil War. Arnold Constable & Company erected its Second Empire extravaganza in 1869, to be followed a year later by Lord & Taylor's similar ornate structure.

Across Broadway, between 18th and 19th Streets, W. & J. Sloane would build something entirely different.

By now the Sloane firm had come a long way from its founding in 1843. William Sloane had learned the craft of weaving in his native Scotland. Nine years after arriving in New York, he opened a store on Broadway across from City Hall where he sold oilcloth floor coverings and carpets. When his brother, John, joined him in 1852, the firm became W. & J. Sloane.

The store had gained a reputation for high-quality goods by the end of the Civil War and catered to New York's carriage trade. With the death of their father and uncle, William's three sons—John, William D., and Henry T.—carried on the business.

Like other businesses, the Sloane company followed the northward march of commerce; moving to 501 Broadway in 1855, to 591 Broadway six years later, then to 649–655 Broadway. In 1881 the Sloanes were ready to relocate again.

Property was purchased on the east side of Broadway, lots 800 through 880, in the city's most fashionable shopping district. Architect William Wheeler Smith was put to work designing a store that would look nothing like any of the surrounding emporiums.

Completed in 1882, it was six stories of brick, stone, cast iron, and terra-cotta that melded Renaissance, Baroque, and Gothic elements into what has been called by some the "Commercial Palace Style." Cornices above the first, third, fifth, and sixth floors accentuated the horizontal, while shallow brick pilasters stretched upward. Smith playfully embellished the façade—particularly within the terracotta capitals of the pilasters—with birds, monsters, angels, and other fantastic figures.

The $400,000 building was termed by *King's Handbook of New York City* as "a solid, graceful edifice" that was "scarcely vast enough for the display of the large

stock dealt in by W. & J. Sloane." The handbook went on to say, "They control the product of a great number of domestic and foreign carpet-mills, and moreover import the best work of other mills of Germany, Switzerland, Scotland, England and France." It was, said King's, "indisputably at the head of the carpet and rug industry of this country."

Not content with their tremendous success in the carpet and rug business, the Sloane brothers branched into related areas: interior design, upholstery, and antiques. Nearly every major hotel in New York—the Waldorf-Astoria, the Plaza, and Savoy among them—was decorated and carpeted by Sloane. When Czar Nicholas II of Russia was crowned, the rugs were supplied by W. & J. Sloane.

The six floors of showrooms were filled with acres of goods. On October 21, 1889, the *New York Times* remarked, "Ladies who visit the store go into ecstasies over the magnificent carpets, tapestries, portieres, and furnishings. They say they really never saw anything like it."

The article listed items such as "attractive brocades for furniture coverings and hangings. One piece has pink roses on a ground of reseda. They are so artistically wrought that they seem to be the actual flowers. A splendid assortment of skins is a feature also. The Mongolian leopard and tiger skins are very fine."

W. & J. Sloane's impressive building was assessed by the deputy tax commissioner in 1892 at $3 million.

W. & J. SLOANE

Hall in Sherry's, New York, showing Berlin Whole Carpets on floor and stairs, made to order by W. & J. Sloane

THE effective key-note in any interior decorative scheme is the floor covering. We feel confident that there is no collection of Imported and Domestic Carpetings in the world which offers a wider range for selection than that which is contained in our establishment. We have also unusual facilities for designing and making

WHOLE CARPETS

which are artistic masterpieces, being woven in one piece, and having an individuality not possessed by carpetings woven in lengths. This is particularly true of the Aubusson, which is really a tapestry applied to floor covering. The French Savonneries, and Chenille Axminsters from Scotch looms, command attention because of their rich tones, and where stronger styles are desired, the Berlin Carpets, woven to special designs exclusively for us, command themselves. All of these carpets may be woven to order to fit any room of irregular outlines.

Broadway and Nineteenth Street, New York

An advertisement pictured the "whole carpet" made to order for the new Sherry's.

Not only did the business provide immense fortunes to the Sloane brothers, but the growth of the company necessitated the addition in 1898 of a nine-story warehouse addition on 19th Street. William Wheeler Smith was once again commissioned to design the harmonious structure.

On December 9, 1905, John Sloane, the president and head of the firm, died. He had been an employee of W. & J. Sloane since he was 15 years old. By now the firm was much more than a carpeting store. In 1906, *Sweet's Indexed Catalogue of Building Construction* said, "W. & J. Sloane have their own corps of designers and decorators, skilled painters, plasterers, fresco workers, carvers, cabinet markets and other artisans to whom any undertaking, whether simple or elaborate, is capable of satisfactory execution. They have their own Wood Working Factory where they make to order Special Design Furniture, as well as Wood Trim of the highest class." The firm employed a staff of over 500 at the time.

The company designed and wove custom-made Aubusson and Beauvais tapestries, curtains and fabrics. Sloane was essentially the sole source for "whole carpets," which would be designed in-house and manufactured at Sloane mills. The company kept a staff in the Middle East to select Oriental rugs to be imported for sale in the Broadway showrooms.

And yet W. & J. Sloane continued to branch out. By 1909 its product line included linoleum for motorboats. On March 25 of that year *Motor Boat* magazine deemed the company the "leading house which furnishes linoleum to the motorboat manufacturers and owners... They make a specialty of it, and are the largest firm, both wholesale and retail in the United States."

As the high-end stores moved up Fifth Avenue, so did W. & J. Sloane, erecting its new headquarters at Fifth Avenue and 47th Street in 1912. The *Dry Goods Reporter* announced that "William Meyer & Company, importers of laces and embroideries, for many years at Broadway and Broome Street, celebrated the opening of their new saleroom, 880-888 Broadway, corner 19th Street, on August 1st."

Sloane leased the W. and J. Sloane building to William Meyer "for a long term of years," and the article went on to say that "the beautiful sales room gave every evidence of the extensive alterations that have been going on for some months past."

William Meyer manufactured and imported embroideries, laces, handkerchiefs, white goods, nets and veilings. It owned mills in Switzerland and was the sole selling agent for certain Irish linens. The firm shared the building with other apparel companies, including Burton, Price & Co., sellers of ribbons, and the necktie firm of Excello Cravats.

By the 1950s, when the New York Pressing Iron Company had its headquarters here, the building was known as the Schwartz Building. That company would continue doing business in the building into the 1970s.

Hurried New Yorkers miss the whimsical and intricate details by simply not looking up.

Brown and red materials combine to form a rich contrast.

At the time that W. & J. Sloane was carpeting the coronation of the Czar and building a new warehouse behind its store, Austrian-born Sam Weinrib was selling used carpeting and linoleum from a pushcart. The immigrant's tiny business was expanded by his son and by 1981, just as W. & J. Sloane had been, was the most prominent name in New York for carpeting and upholstery—ABC Carpet & Home.

That year ABC purchased the old Sloane building and renovated it, treating the historic façade with care. The firm is still there today, the largest importer and retailer of wool carpeting in the United States. It is an amazingly appropriate use for the former carpeting showroom; a stunning building which, upon its completion, was nominated as one of the "best ten buildings" in America.

CENTURY ASSOCIATION BUILDING

109–111 EAST 15TH STREET

In 1847 when The Century Club was founded—taking its name from the 100 invited members—Union Square was developing as a most fashionable residential district. The park was ringed with fine brick homes and churches, which spilled onto the side streets— all except for East 15th Street, where five industrial buildings created a stark exception.

The five buildings were faced by two wooden homes across the street to the north, one being No. 42 East 15th Street. That two-and-a-half-story house was purchased in 1855 by Isaac Lewis, a builder. Before long the house and the block would change dramatically.

In 1857 the Century Club became incorporated as the Century Association, a social organization for authors, artists, and dabblers in the fine arts. The *Sun* would praise the club as having "a purpose to serve," unlike those that had for their "principal end the affording to young men of conveniences for idle amusement." Instead, the proper Victorian gentlemen set as their goal "plain living and high thinking."

The club had bounced from location to location until that year, when it increased its membership to 250. With a permanent clubhouse now deemed a necessity, the Century purchased No. 42 from Lewis for $24,000.

Club member and architect Joseph C. Wells set about renovating the wooden house into a proper clubhouse. The $11,000 renovations resulted in a Cinderella-like transformation. The frame house became an Italian palazzo with a balustraded staircase and pedimented windows.

Throughout the Civil War years the club continued to grow and expand its activities. The clubhouse, by 1866, was no longer adequate for its functions and meetings. A committee was formed to decide whether to move or renovate the building.

It was a time of financial uncertainty for exclusive men's clubs. The eminent Union Club was reported to be "deep in debt" by the *Sun* and the New York Club had heavily borrowed to keep afloat. Before long, both the Athenaeum and the Eclectic Club would close due to financial hardship.

Considering its finances, the Century opted to renovate. Charles D. Gambrill and George B. Post, partners in the architectural firm of Gambrill & Post, were both club members. In May of the following year Gambrill submitted his proposal for renovations.

For some unexplained reason, part of Gambrill's design—an extension to the rear of the clubhouse—was quickly completed; but the interior alterations and the new façade sat on the drafting table. The new extension provided for a billiard room on the main floor and an art gallery above.

During the two years while the plans collected dust, Post left the architectural firm and Gambrill took on Henry Hobson Richardson who, like Post, would go on to be ranked among America's preeminent nineteenth-century architects.

Finally in 1869 construction began under plans filed by Gambrill & Richardson. The amount of input Richardson had in the final designs is undocumented; but whichever architect was responsible, the result was noteworthy.

Gone was the Italian palazzo with its stone balustraded fences and Renaissance-styled windows. In its place appeared a brick and stone neo-Grec structure with a formal countenance that reflected the propriety of the club members. The third-floor attic was raised to form a full-floor mansard. Stone courses doubled as structural support and horizontal design elements. The completed renovations cost $21,000—nearly the full price the club paid for the building originally. The renovated clubhouse was deemed by the *Sun* "a handsome and commodious house… where its members believed it had found a permanent place of abode."

The Century Association would see America's brightest literary and artistic figures sign their membership rolls throughout the years. The unending list included actor Edwin Booth, and artists Albert Bierstadt, Frederic Church, Charles C. Tiffany, and Augustus Saint-Gaudens. Politicians such as Grover Cleveland, Theodore Roosevelt, and Hamilton Fish were members; as were William Cullen Bryant, all three members of the architectural firm McKim, Mead & White, and millionaires John Jacob Astor, Jr., Cornelius Vanderbilt, and J. Pierpont Morgan.

By 1887 when the guidebook *How to Know New York City* called the Century Association "a literary, artistic, and aesthetic club, with… a large library, and a picture-gallery," membership had grown to 600.

That same year sculptor Auguste Bartholdi arrived in New York to help raise money for the pedestal of his *Liberty Enlightening the World*. The colossal statue had been presented to the United States as a gift from the people of France; however, it might well have included a tag: "base not included." Bartholdi understandably chose the Century Association building for his January 2, 1877, fundraising speech.

As the century entered its last decade, Union Square had become a center of commerce, its splendid homes having been razed for business buildings. Although the Century Association had expected that its clubhouse—now renumbered Nos. 109–111 East 15th Street—would be its "permanent abode," on January 12, 1890, the *Sun* reported that "the conservative old club has finally determined to follow the march of things up town."

One year later, almost to the day, the Century, now with 800 members, took possession of its McKim, Mead & White-designed clubhouse on West 43rd Street.

Before the end of the year the United States Brewers' Association had taken over the old building.

The Association, formed in 1862, now had a membership of about 1,000 throughout the U.S. The group, according to *King's Handbook of New York City* in 1892 sought "protection of its industry from prohibitory and unduly stringent laws, and cooperates with the Government in the execution of the laws pertaining to malt liquors."

The Temperance Movement had swept the country and, in reaction, the Association put a spin on its product. It asserted the seemingly contradictory concept that the drinking of beer reduced indulgence in alcohol. "It is contended by the Association that the industry it represents is in the interest of

King's Handbook of New York City published the above photograph in 1892.

temperance and morality, as its effect is to diminish the consumption of intoxicating liquors," said the *Handbook*.

Unlike the Century Association before it, the Brewers' Association had political goals on its agenda. In December 1898 a "congress" of brewers from across the United States was held to call upon Congress to abolish the war tax on beer. During the Spanish-American War both the saloon keeper and the consumer paid a tax to help offset war expenses.

"Now the peace treaty is about to be signed and the first thing that should be done to relieve the people is the abolishment of this tax," said a speaker. "The people" were common Americans, he contended. "The tax affects the farmer as well as the brewer."

The *Sun* was more interested in the members than the purpose of the congress. When millionaires were mentioned, it was bankers and railroad moguls who came to mind. But many beer brewers had amassed enormous fortunes. "This will be the first time in the history of this or any other city where so many millionaires have gathered at one hall at the same time," the newspaper predicted. It estimated the aggregate worth of the delegates to be over $400 million.

The ire of dignified socialites and religious leaders was no doubt raised when they read accounts of a meeting here on December 18, 1901. A resolution was passed that read, in part, "It is the sense of this board that a law permitting in the City of New York the sale of liquors, ales, wine and beer on Sunday, between the hours of 1 P.M. and 11 P.M., is one consonant with the needs of this community."

Justice William Travers Jerome spoke out saying, "Once realizing the facts, I do not see how any thinking man can believe that I am not right in my view of this question. Some 200,000 of the population of this city want to be able to secure liquor on Sunday, and I do not see that it is my province, or anyone else's to prescribe a code of morals for so considerable a body of citizens, whatever may be our personal desires as to drinking on Sundays."

It was just the sort of added stimulation the Prohibitionists were looking for, and 1901 saw increased activity in the Temperance movement.

In 1914 the Brewers' Association fired back at the Temperance leaders, publishing an advertisement disguising itself as an educational list in *The World Almanac & Book of Facts*. Included in the long list were assertions that:

— *A marked decrease in drunkenness has been noted as a result of the increased sales of beer.*
— *Prohibition has gained little or no headway in New York State notwithstanding the persistent and continued activities on the part of the various prohibition organizations.*
— *The traffic in alcoholic beverages pays an annual direct tax of nearly $20,000,000 to the State of New York in addition to other taxes; more than one-third of the entire State Budget.*

The advertisement did not work.

In September 1918 the Fuel Administration issued an order prohibiting the brewing of beer after December 1. A meeting at the United States Brewers' Association building was immediately called. The ramifications of the order were far-reaching.

There were 9,673 saloons in the five boroughs. Their closing would mean tens of thousands of New Yorkers would lose their employment—there were at the time around 25,000 bartenders alone. The breweries had enormous reserve stocks of grain and other ingredients; not to mention the thousands of barrels of beer stored in gigantic tanks.

Then, on January 16, 1919, the 18th Amendment to the Constitution was ratified prohibiting the "manufacture, sale, or transportation of intoxicating liquors" and on October 28 of that year the Volstead Act was passed to enforce the new laws.

The Women's Christian Temperance Union, the major player in the movement, had gotten its way. In doing so they left jobless "middle-aged and elderly men still in the business in which they have always worked," as described by the *New York Times*.

With only minor alterations, the building survives much as it appeared in the 1890s.

They also put an end to the United States Brewers' Association.

For a few years the Interboro Mutual Indemnity Insurance Company, originally organized in 1914 as the Brewers Mutual Indemnity Insurance Company, stayed on in the building. Then, throughout the 20th century the old clubhouse saw a variety of uses. In the 1920s it became home to the Manhattan chapter of the Sons of Italy Hall, and in the 1930s the Galicia Sporting Club.

Eventually No. 109–111 East 15th Street was occupied by the New York Joint Board of Shirt, Leisurewear, Robe and Sportswear Workers Union; then an Asian-American trading company that also ran a dry-cleaning shop in the basement.

In 1996 a year-long restoration and renovation of the building was initiated by Beyer Blinder Belle, transforming the former clubhouse into the Century Center for the Performing Arts. The new facility included a 248-seat theater, a studio, and a ballroom.

After a decade it was taken over as the New York City production facility for the world's largest religious television network, Trinity Broadcasting Network. The company offers 24 hours of commercial-free programming aimed at Protestant, Catholic, and Jewish audiences.

With minor alterations (the iron cresting of the roof is gone, as are the entrance steps, and the basement windows are now doorways), the distinguished clubhouse is mainly unchanged. It was designated a New York City landmark in 1993.

GRAMERCY

THE GEORGE W. BELLOWS HOUSE
146 E. 19TH STREET

THEODORE ROOSEVELT HOUSE
28 E. 20TH STREET

THE LITTLE GOTHIC HOUSE
129 E. 19TH STREET

GEORGE W. BELLOWS HOUSE
146 EAST 19TH STREET

In 1831, Samuel B. Ruggles hatched an ambitious plan for an elegant private park lined with mansions on what had been part of James Duane's Gramercy Farm. By the 1850s the blocks surrounding Gramercy Park were quickly developing. On East 19th Street between Irving Place and Third Avenue, just one block south of the park, three-story Greek Revival homes lined the street. Most of them were clad in brick and shared similar architectural features. They were constructed for financially comfortable, but not wealthy, buyers.

No. 146 East 19th Street was home to John Baker and his wife. The joy from the birth of their son, Sperry, came to a tragic end when the infant died on Sunday, March 19, 1855. Two days later the baby's funeral was held in the parlor here.

Jane Farrell was living in the house in 1873. She had an unpleasant run-in with James Anderson on August 13 of that year when the crook snatched her pocketbook containing $23. Anderson was caught and in court pleaded innocent to stealing the purse because it had been recovered. He pled guilty, instead, to "an attempt."

Nevertheless, he was sent to the penitentiary for two years.

Fifteen years later, the house was being used as the office of what its advertisements called "the old and celebrated Medical Institute." Claiming to have cured 15,000 men "in a few years," the questionable Institute promised to heal numerous male sexual problems. An advertisement placed in the *Sun* on December 1, 1889, boasted, "All secret and private diseases of men cured in a few days; no charge unless cured; health, lost manhood restored; suffer no longer; cure is certain; bear in mind practice makes perfect."

How long the Medical Institute stayed in the house is unclear; however, by the turn of the century, Mrs. Anna L. Christensen ran her Swedish Employment Bureau from here with her partner, Miss Mina S. Johnson. The women helped newly arrived Swedes find respectable employment in their new country.

The Bureau was in the house through 1909, after which it once again became a private home. In 1910 artist George W. Bellows purchased it. At the time architect Frederick Junius Sterner had already begun transforming many of the old houses on

Although unfortunately painted, the house retains much of its original detailing.

Bellows captured the energy of the metropolis in his 1911 *New York City.*

the street into up-to-date homes in fanciful Tudor, Gothic, and Mediterranean styles. The block quickly attracted artistic residents like Robert Chanler and actresses Ethel Barrymore, Helen Hayes, and the Gish sisters.

Unlike some of his neighbors, Bellows did not give his pre-Civil War home a facelift. He opted to retain the old Greek Revival design while he raised the upper floor 8 feet to accommodate his studio and installed an expansive skylight-type window. The brownstone stoop was replaced with one of brick.

Bellows and his wife, the former Emma Story, had two daughters while they were living in the house—Ann, born in 1912, and Jean in 1915. The paintings that emerged from the top-floor studio drew both praise and protest.

The *New York Times* remarked, "He painted from life and from imagination, using a great variety of themes." His gritty New York City pictures like *The Cliff Dwellers* represented tenement life with no excuses and raised "wide interest," according to the newspaper. He captured the moment when boxer Jack Dempsey was knocked through the ropes by Firpo. When he exhibited his *Nude Girl With a Shawl* at the National Arts Club Exhibition in 1915, it drew protests as "too realistic."

Nevertheless, he earned recognition and awards year after year. While still living and working on 19th Street, he saw his paintings purchased by the Brooklyn Museum, the Columbus Art Association, the Metropolitan Museum of Art, the National Arts Club, the Detroit Museum, the Cleveland Museum, the Albright, and the Phillips Memorial Gallery in Washington, among many others.

In 1918, Bellows was selected to join in an exhibition to benefit the Fourth Liberty Loan drive. New York-based painters and sculptors donated their work "in order to persuade the public to the utmost of zeal in buying bonds and putting an end to bondage," said the *New York Times* on October 6.

Bellows's way of persuading bond purchase was to expose to the public the atrocities of war. The newspaper's art critic wrote, "George Bellows has made use of every agency for the communication of horror in his picture 'The Germans Arrive.' Prussian officers are cutting off the hands of a lad and throttling a woman; other atrocities are indicated in the subsidiary groups. The treatment is characteristic and familiar to a public acquainted with the artist's pugilist subjects. Long practice in realistic illustration of scenes of physical violence has made possible a convincing report at second hand of what we have all heard."

Like every other artist, Bellows had to pay the bills. To supplement the sales of his more creative works, he painted portraits of society women—a stark contrast to so many of his gritty, earthier subjects.

On Friday, January 2, 1925, the 43-year-old artist fell ill in his studio. Struck with appendicitis, he was rushed to the Post Graduate Hospital where he was operated on the following day. Five days later, on January 8, he died in the hospital.

Emma and the two girls stayed on in the 19th Street house. Bellows's works, already highly regarded (the *Times* called him "one of America's most distinguished painters"), soared in value. His *Emma and Her Children*, formerly valued at $3,000, was sold to the Boston Museum shortly after his death for $22,000.

When Jean married on December 11, 1949, at the age of 35, Emma was left alone in the house on 19th Street. In May 1955 the aging widow sold the house to the New York Investors Mutual Group. It appeared to be the end of the line for the historic home. The *New York Times* reported that, "The site will be incorporated with other holdings for improvement with an apartment building."

But someone changed his mind. A year later the house was converted to two apartments—a duplex on the first and second floors, and another in the third and "mezzanine"—George Bellows's sun-drenched art studio.

In 1956 one of the apartments was leased by Anne Lindbergh, wife of the famous aviator Charles Lindbergh. According to biographers, she used the Manhattan *pied a terre* not only as a getaway from their Connecticut home and a place for seeing friends, but also as a place of rendezvous with her physician and lover, Dr. Dana Atchley.

Today, the house remains unchanged, albeit unfortunately covered in barn-red paint. From its uppermost floors emerged some of America's modern art masterpieces—a broad swath encompassing sweating athletes to earthy urban landscapes to refined society portraits.

THEODORE ROOSEVELT HOUSE

28 EAST 20TH STREET

In 1848 the six matching brownstone houses at Nos. 18 through 28 East 20th Street, built on speculation, were choice properties. Sitting about half-way between Fifth Avenue and fashionable Gramercy Park, their staid Gothic Revival exteriors hinted at the social and financial status of those living inside; although almost six decades later, in 1905, the *New York Times* would remember the block as "in a location respectable, though not 'swell.'"

By now, the Roosevelt family had been in New York for two centuries and had accumulated substantial wealth and social importance. Theodore and Robert Roosevelt purchased the new houses at Nos. 28 and 26, respectively. Theodore, a lawyer, married Martha "Mittie" Bulloch five years later. His brother Robert was a publisher.

Theodore and Mittie started their family in No. 28 with the birth of little Anna Roosevelt. Soon after came the first boy, Theodore Roosevelt, Jr., born on October 27, 1858. There would be another son and daughter.

Little Theodore was asthmatic and sickly. Confined mostly to the East 20th Street house, he developed an acute interest in zoology. That interest was reportedly sparked when, at the age of seven, he saw a dead seal at a market and brought the head home. With two of his cousins he started what they called the "Roosevelt Museum of Natural History."

He taught himself the basics of taxidermy, and his little museum exhibited stuffed animals he had killed and prepared. By the time he was nine he had documented his study of insects in a paper titled "The Natural History of Insects." Much to his delight, the backyard of the Peter Goelet mansion on Broadway, behind the Roosevelt house, held a menagerie of cows, pheasants, storks, and other exotic animals.

Despite his son's sometimes life-threatening illnesses, Theodore, Sr., did not coddle the boy. He installed an outdoor gymnasium for his frail, nearsighted son and told him, "Theodore, you have the mind but you have not the body, and without the help of the body, the mind cannot go as far as it should. I am giving you the tools, but it is up to you to make your body."

Home-schooled by tutors, little Theodore Roosevelt developed both his mind and body at No. 28 East 20th Street. He did breathing and strength exercises in the back yard and began boxing. It was here that his championing of "the strenuous life" started.

His father's influence went beyond the physical. Teddy would say of him later, "My father, Theodore Roosevelt, was the best man I ever knew. He combined strength and courage with gentleness, tenderness, and great unselfishness. He would not tolerate in us children selfishness or cruelty, idleness, cowardice, or untruthfulness."

In 1873, when Teddy was fourteen years old, the family left No. 28 East 20th. The home was immediately

Few passersby would guess that the house has been heavily rebuilt.

converted to a rooming house, and in 1874 an advertisement in the *New York Times* offered "two handsomely furnished front rooms on the second floor."

Various advertisements would appear throughout the next two decades. With most well-to-do families away for the summer on July 19, 1880, an ad in the *New-York Tribune* offered "rooms to let, with or without board, at very low summer prices. References."

The advertisement in the same newspaper on August 19, 1886, was apparently successful, for it ran verbatim for years: "At 28 East 20th-ST., near Broadway— Handsomely furnished rooms for gentlemen; first-class attendance."

By 1894, Dr. Elmer P. Arnold had established his practice here, most probably on the basement level. He hired as his nurse Mrs. Ellen A. Clayton, who lived conveniently nearby at 37 East 20th Street. Ellen made a shopping trip to one of the Sixth Avenue emporiums on January 11, 1895. A few inexpensive items caught her eye so she took them. Literally.

Unfortunately for Ellen, a store detective noticed her stuff a pair of 60-cent gloves in her pocket. She was arrested with goods totaling less than $3.00 on her. Amazingly, she had $116.16 in cash in her purse—nearly $3,000 in today's money. When the Sergeant at the West 13th Street Station asked her why she stole the items, "She told the Sergeant she thought she must be crazy," reported the *Times*.

In 1898 the Roosevelt family, who still held the property, stripped off part of the brownstone façade and erected an ungainly glass and metal storefront. Just before New Year's Day in 1898 the Wendell Dining Rooms opened, a restaurant that boasted a French chef "and superior appointments."

The Wendell Dining Rooms would last only a year or two. The Roosevelts sold the house, oddly enough still described as a "four-story dwelling," to William R. Kendall in 1899. Coexisting with the variety of businesses in the building were a few residential tenants. In 1900 artist Paul Nimmo Moran was living here.

Following McKinley's assassination in 1901, Theodore Roosevelt became President of the United States. Early in October 1904, during Roosevelt's winning campaign, a group of Republicans from the 17th Election District "formulated the plan of holding meetings in a 'hallowed spot,'" as reported in the *New York Times* on October 21. The new organization called itself the Roosevelt Club and leased the only room available in the Roosevelt birthplace.

The *Times* said, "It was found that the only space available was the rear room on the top floor, four flights up from the street." Nevertheless the group took the space and "got to work to decorate the little room, which is about 6 feet by 9, with flags and lithographs of the Republican candidates."

Until the night of their first meeting, there was considerable debate among New Yorkers as to whether the highly-altered building at 20 West 28th Street was even the President's actual birthplace. All questions were put to rest when a telegram from the White House arrived at the clubroom which read:

"Permit me to extend my hearty congratulations on the occasion of the meeting of the club in the house where I was born. THEODORE ROOSEVELT."

By 1919 the once-proud residence had been even more severely altered. In March the *New York Times* noted, "Before the house was sold several years ago for commercial uses it was a four-story brownstone, but alterations to make it useful for a restaurant and shops made it of only two stories."

The house and the adjoining John E. and Robert Roosevelt house were purchased for a group of concerned women, calling themselves the Women's Roosevelt Memorial Committee. The *Times* said, "When the Women's Memorial Committee was organized, one of the first proposals made to it was that the birthplace of the twenty-sixth President should be bought and preserved for posterity as many other houses of famous men born in this city have been preserved."

The purchasers were represented by the Douglas Robinson, Charles E. Brown Company. The Robinson family was related to Theodore Roosevelt by marriage.

Popular lore today often insists that the house had been leveled and the Memorial Committee was charged with reproducing the house from scratch. Although the house was heavily altered, tales of its complete demolition, like Mark Twain's premature obituary, are greatly exaggerated.

The *Times* noted that because of the state of the building, "the interior will have to be restored entirely," and, "In restoring the house, the descriptions to be furnished by members of the family will be followed closely, as well as the description written by Colonel Roosevelt in his autobiography."

In announcing its plans, the Committee said, "With its assembly halls to be visited by people from all over the country who loved him and who would study the influences that made up his growth, it is to be made a centre of citizenship activities, a place where all citizens can come together in order that their understanding of America may become deeper and keener. Colonel Roosevelt's vigor of life, robustness of belief and energy of will are the real background of this memorial."

The group established a goal of $1 million and fundraising started immediately. In October Major General Leonard Wood delivered an address at Carnegie Hall; pledges from the Boy Scouts and Girl Scouts of America flowed in; and William Webster Ellsworth gave an illustrated lecture on "Theodore Roosevelt—American." The *New-York Tribune*, on April 27, 1920, ran an advertisement reading: "Men and Women of America are asked to help restore the birthplace of Theodore Roosevelt."

The Memorial Committee commissioned female architect Theodate Pope Riddle to oversee the restoration. Riddle used the Robert Roosevelt house, an exact copy, as a pattern for the new house museum. The Gothic Revival drip moldings, the marvelous row of arches beneath the cornice, the floor-to-ceiling parlor windows opening onto the cast-iron balcony, and the fish-scale tiled mansard roof were all reproduced.

Then, having used the house at No. 26 for its details, she promptly obliterated them. More than half a century later the Landmarks Preservation Commission would diplomatically say she "subordinated the features of the Robert Roosevelt house in order to enhance the importance of Theodore Roosevelt's birthplace." In fact, seeing no historical importance in that building, Riddle replaced it with a flat, featureless wall with windows. As would be expected in the 1920s, the *Times* saw nothing wrong in the unsympathetic conversion.

"The house next door, where Roosevelt played much as a boy, as it belonged to his uncle, Robert Barnwell Roosevelt, a prominent Democratic politician in his day and American Minister to Holland under President Cleveland, has been designed for a museum and library."

THE ROOSEVELT HOUSE, 28 East Twentieth Street
New York
The adjoining house, No. 26, contains
the Library and Historical Museum

In 1923, the Theodore Roosevelt House emerged like new; the Robert Roosevelt house was decimated.

Roosevelt's widow, Edith, and his two sisters donated original furnishings. Rooms were outfitted to reflect the house as it appeared in 1865. By October 1922 the Committee had received contributions totaling $1.9 million and collected thousands of items related to Roosevelt. The house contained five period rooms, two museum galleries, and a bookstore.

The house was finally completed and dedicated on October 27, 1923. Twentieth Street was roped off and "hung with American flags," and amplifiers carried the addresses to the crowd of 600 outside.

The *New York Times* described the period rooms that "will be thrown open to the public, replete with exhibits touching on his life from birth to death." It reported: "The parlor of the home itself contains the original furniture, and the dining room table is that used by the family of the Colonel. This room and the library

A mid-century postcard shows the bedroom where the President was born.

are furnished for the most part with reproductions of the original furniture. The front bedroom, where Colonel Roosevelt was born, is furnished with the original bedroom set, family portraits decorating the walls. The nursery at the rear has some originals. The library has many first editions, many of them autographed, of Colonel Roosevelt's books. The roof is given over to a garden where lunches and dinners will be served."

For years the Woman's Roosevelt Memorial Association presented a bronze medallion at an annual reception in the house. On January 4, 1933, it was Amelia Earhart who was awarded the medal, which bore a portrait of Roosevelt.

In 1963 the house was donated to the National Park Service, and it was listed on the National Register of Historic Places on October 15, 1966. Few passersby would suspect that the prim brownstone-fronted house suffered serious abuse a century ago and that little is original. The Roosevelt House is a remarkably early example of historic preservation, especially considering the monumental task the women who envisioned it had before them.

THE LITTLE GOTHIC HOUSE

129 EAST 19TH STREET

When the wealthy James Couper Lord, a dealer in iron, purchased Charles Moran's Gramercy Park home in 1855, the rear lot facing 19th Street was still a grassy plot. It would remain so for another six years before Lord had a two-story carriage house constructed in 1861.

It is not known if James C. Lord used his stable for anything else, however, before the turn of the century it had been converted into the studio of stained-glass craftsman Craig F. R. Drake. Just when the stable took on its charming Gothic Revival costume is undocumented. The picturesque, protruding entrance formed a crenellated balcony for the second-story arched double doors. Flat-headed Gothic eyebrows floated oddly above shallow-arched windows and a Gothic scallop was affixed below the modest cornice.

Drake would stay on in the little building for several years; an advertisement in the April 20, 1901, issue of the *Churchman* listed him as a "glass stainer" of memorial windows. Craig was, according to the *New York Times* years later, responsible for the leaded, diamond-pattern windows.

In 1903 author and artist F. Berkeley Smith leased the building and had architect

Where ironwork now crests the entrance there was originally wooden crenellation.

Nichols in 1897 (left) and in 1922 when he was living at No. 129.

August Pauli design interior renovations, creating residential space. Although Smith most likely spent more time traveling than at home (he wrote and illustrated numerous books about foreign cities), he created a comfortable two-bedroom home outfitted with wood paneling and fireplaces. That same year the *New York Times* complimented the little house at 129 East 19th Street as having the most "picturesque exterior" in all of New York.

By 1909 the building was the office of architect Herbert Lucas and construction engineer Colonel Eugene Willett Van Court Lucas. But it would be a residence again before long.

After graduating from Harvard, writer Humphrey Turner Nichols was living with his wife, Edith, and their two small children at 16 Gramercy Park. In 1912 he said humbly of his career, "I have done little which deserves the chronicling. An occasional splutter in the newspaper columns and a little hack work."

But by 1917, Nichols, whose great-grandfather was an *aide-de-camp* to General George Washington and who was a member of the Society of Mayflower Descendants, was listing 129 East 19th Street as his business address. The family owned a summer house in York Harbor, Maine, and now he was the secretary of the Players Club on Gramercy Park. He wrote of that post: "This very delightful occupation brings me into constant contact with the noted painters, sculptors, writers, playwrights, musicians, and actors of the day."

By 1922 Nichols had moved his office to 45 East 17th Street and made East 19th Street his home. When he was not writing or at the Players Club, he was a member of the Union and Harvard Clubs in New York, and the Tennis & Racquet Club in Boston.

Four years later Humphrey and Edith Nichols moved to Boston. The pretty little house would see a quick succession of tenants. In 1931 the widow of Aldo R. Balsam, Margaret Nash Balsam, leased the house. Two years later it was the scene of resident William Henry Hamilton's wedding to Anne Kirkpatrick. Hamilton was a member of the Council of New York University and the president of the Travelers

The flat Gothic eyebrows float mysteriously over window openings that do not match.

Aid Society. Like Nichols, he was a clubman, having memberships in the University, Turf and Field, Piping Rock, City Midday, and Riding Clubs.

The *Times* reported that the newlyweds "after a wedding trip in Europe, will divide their time between this city and Mr. Hamilton's country place in St. James, Long Island."

Dr. Marvin B. Day leased the house in October 1941, and exactly two years later it was leased to Charles Chase by Dr. Clara Day.

Richard Dudensing, III, and his wife, June, were living here in October 1949 when their daughter Judy was born. Both father and mother came from well-established New York families.

Four years later, the owner, Mrs. Gertrude H. Calfee, sold the house to Florence R. Frost. By this time a third story had been added. It was assessed at the time for $45,000. The charming little storybook home survived throughout the 20th century, catching the eye of tourist and New Yorker alike.

When the house sold again in 1992, a restoration of sorts was executed with the input of the Landmarks Preservation Commission. Because there seems to be no documentation on the original renovations and how the little carriage house became a Gothic gingerbread house, its architectural history is somewhat mysterious.

But none of that detracts from the end product: a delightful and surprising little house.

FLATIRON DISTRICT

SPERO BUILDING
19 - 27 WEST 21ST STREET

FLATIRON BUILDING
23RD AT BROADWAY
AND FIFTH AVENUE

REFINED REMNANTS, 178-180 FIFTH AVENUE

The hefty industrial structure is embellished with sturdy Art Nouveau elements.

SPERO BUILDING
19–27 WEST 21ST STREET

At the turn of the last century the block on 21st Street between Fifth and Sixth Avenues saw a burst of development. The high-end brownstone homes of a generation earlier were quickly razed, to be replaced by tall manufacturing loft buildings. The shipping and receiving entrances of many of the large 23rd Street retail stores were located in the rear, on 22nd Street. The resulting traffic made 21st Street more desirable for light manufactory buildings. In January 1908 the *New York Times* remarked, "This block on Twenty-first Street has shown unusually steady growth."

Stern Brothers Department Store was one of the large emporiums on 23rd Street. Several years before the *Times* article was written, Benjamin Stern had acquired the string of properties from 19 to 27 West 21st Street. His intention was to open an annex connected to the main store by a tunnel. Although the tunnel was built and was being used for the delivery of stock from 21st Street, the plan to build the annex was abandoned as the block rapidly filled with mercantile buildings rather than retail establishments.

In 1907, Stern sold the 104-foot-wide property to developer David Spero, who planned a modern loft building for the site. The *New York Times* reported that, "One of the few large gaps remaining in the rows of tall loft buildings on Twenty-first Street, between Fifth and Sixth Avenues, will soon be closed by the new twelve-story structure." Spero commissioned architect Robert D. Kohn to design the building.

In April of that year Kohn's magnificent headquarters for the *Evening Post* was completed (see page 14). This was exceptional among Manhattan buildings in that Kohn strayed from the safety of Beaux Arts and Renaissance-inspired architecture and looked across the ocean to the groundbreaking Art Nouveau style. The *Evening Post* building was a bold expression of Art Nouveau's Vienna Secession offshoot. For David Spero's new building, Kohn would go back to that well.

Completed in 1908 at a cost of around $350,000, the building featured a muscular façade clad in gray brick, limestone, and granite. Kohn ornamented the building with hefty two-story piers at the base that terminated in fountain-like Art Nouveau

The Spero Building as it appeared one year after completion.

carvings. In between, copper-roofed oriel windows added light to the interior and created an undulating movement to the façade. The irregular roofline and the verticality of the uppermost floors, which protruded slightly from the lower surface supported by metal brackets, reflected the Vienna Secession influence.

The neighborhood had already become the center of the apparel industry, and quickly the building filled with garment firms. B. Altman & Co. took 10,000 feet on the second floor in 1908; Turkel & Felstiner was another early tenant.

Rosenberg & Co. was here in 1911 when one of its employees went missing. Although the poorly paid girls in the garment factories were very often nearly illiterate immigrants, 22-year-old Hannah Reiner was educated and a lover of books. During the summer months the Bronx resident would often hire a rowboat during her time off, row far out onto a lake in a park, then drift lazily along lost in a book.

On Tuesday, June 13, she did just that. At 3:45 she rented a boat from Grosse's boathouse in Pelham Bay Park and left her valuables for safekeeping—a pocketbook containing letters and $1.35, her white silk parasol, and some other articles—then rowed out onto the bay with a copy of Shakespeare's *Julius Caesar*.

It was the last time anyone would see her alive.

When Hannah failed to return for dinner, her mother became alarmed and sent her brother to find her. The rowboat was found, without its oars, with the girl's book on the floor. As days passed, the police dragged the bay to no avail. "Relatives of the girl believe that as she sat in her rowboat reading a novel some men in a motor boat swooped down upon her and dragged her into their craft," reported the *Evening World* on July 21. "It is believed that some vicious character observed the girl's habit and lay in wait for her."

The following day the same newspaper reported, "Hannah Reiner Slain by Motor Boat Thugs." The article said that her body "was found this afternoon cast upon the beach at Throgg's Neck. The police discovered marks of violence upon the arms and face that indicated that she had been the victim of a mysterious murder."

The coroner's physician reported finding "many cuts and bruises. A deep cut appeared on the head. The arms were bruised and there was a depression on one side of the head that seemed to have been made by a blow."

Hannah Reiner worked in the Spero Building as a dressmaker when she disappeared.

Amazingly, one day later on July 23, the police and the coroner made a 360-degree reversal. The *Sun* reported that, "The police and Coroner are convinced that the young woman fell out of the boat in which she was rowing and that her death was an accident." The marks of violence were suddenly forgotten. "The clothing was not torn and the body showed no bruises or marks."

Although the family vehemently argued that there was foul play involved, the case of Hannah Reiner was abruptly closed.

Earlier that year, the tragic Triangle Shirtwaist fire had resulted in the horrific deaths of 146 garment workers (see page 62). A year later, on March 21, the memory of that tragedy was fresh in the minds of girls making women's waists, or fitted shirts, at the M. I. Nathan Company in the Spero Building. Forty-year-old Julia Gaillard went to the back room to brew a cup of tea over a small gas stove. As she turned, her dress caught fire and the flames rapidly enveloped her clothing and seared her face.

"Screaming frantically, the girl began to race madly down the long aisle, the fire lapping out to threaten all the piles of cloth and paper patterns," reported the *Evening World*. Although a clerk, Isadore Nash, wrapped the woman in an overcoat and snuffed out the flames, it was too late to control the panic among the hundred other workers. The *World* said, "Remembering the Triangle fire, they began a mad scramble for the elevators. Their panic was contagious and within five minutes several hundred more fear-mad women were clawing each other at every angle of the stairway from the second to the twelfth floor."

The two elevator boys, Joe Lowrey and Joe Paul, ran the cars up and down nonstop, attempting to take as many as possible at a time and trying to ensure the women that there was no fire. "Meanwhile, all the building, from top to sidewalk, had caught the infection of panic," said the *Evening World.* "The stairs became jammed almost immediately, and those who heard the cry of 'Fire!' on the upper floors and rushed to the stairways found them clogged by those who were already fleeing in blind terror. The fire escapes on the back of the building became black with girls. Some threw open the windows on the Twenty-first Street side of the building and screamed for rescue to those in the street."

Although order was eventually restored, Julia Gaillard's burns proved fatal.

In 1914 the prominent clothing manufacturer Joseph Jonasson & Co. contemplated leaving the Spero Building for "a new home in the uptown neighborhood." In its

The structure's name is carved boldly into stone above the entrance.

announcement, the firm seemed nearly apologetic. "The Spero Building is not so very old and it is in the district close to Fifth Avenue, where the manufacturing houses flocked a number of years ago, and while its equipment and arrangement cannot be criticized, Joseph Jonasson & Co. have found that the increasing demands of their trade make it imperative that new and larger quarters be secured."

American Cloak and Suit Review reported, "There is no house in the entire industry that is more respected and esteemed than the Jonasson institution." The Spero management was no doubt nervous about losing one of its better-known tenants. Yet the building continued to be filled with similar firms.

In 1916, Jacob Liss, "manufacturers of ladies' waists," moved in, followed by the W. & B. Dress Company on the tenth floor. During the 1920s there were new tenants such as the Champion Cloak Company and the S. J. Hartsfeld Co., which made "boys' wash suits." Superior Stitching Company took the sixth floor in 1927.

As the garment district migrated northward to Seventh Avenue, the Spero Building saw a more varied tenant list. In 1935 Orion Press was here and in the 1940s so was Berton Plastics. Today, an even great variety of renters can be found from Pangloss Films, the documentary film production company founded by filmmaker Peter Yost, to an acupuncturist office. On the ground floor is a massive costume shop, Abracadabra.

Richard Kohn's masculine Art Nouveau design, reflective of the manufacturing nature of the building, is nearly unaltered a century after completion. It is a remarkable example of a style of architecture rarely seen in New York City.

FLATIRON BUILDING

23RD STREET AT BROADWAY AND
FIFTH AVENUE

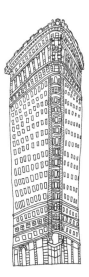

It was not the soaring height of the Fuller Building that caught New Yorkers' attention in 1902. And it was not the masterful, almost sculptural, design. It was the wind.

The pie-shaped plot of land bounded by East 22nd Street, Broadway, and Fifth Avenue—with its nose poking against 23rd Street—held a hodgepodge of small commercial buildings prior to 1902. But its visible location at the confluence of the major arteries coupled with its location across from Madison Square Park gave it an untapped and inestimable value—this despite the neighborhood's recent slide from carriage-trade emporiums to mostly loft spaces with small manufacturing.

The site had been owned by Amos Eno, and after his death in 1899 his son William purchased it from the estate for $690,000, a staggering sum at the turn of the century. Within a month he sold the property to Samuel and Mott Newhouse for $801,000—around $18 million today. Although the Newhouse brothers had lofty plans for the site initially, they eventually sold it to Harry S. Black two years later.

Black ran the Fuller Company, a general contracting company whose specialty was the construction of skyscrapers. In fact Fuller was the first actual "general contractor"—a firm that handled all phases of construction other than its architecture.

Harry S. Black envisioned an impressive new headquarters for his firm—one that would establish not only its reputation as a serious player in the building game, but which would advertise its construction capabilities. Rather than tap the talents of local architects like McKim, Mead & White or Carrère & Hastings, Black turned to Chicago-based Daniel Burnham.

Burnham designed a 21-floor show-stopper, mixing Renaissance Revival with Beaux Arts styles. The façade was slathered with carvings and molded terra-cotta—barely a square foot could be found without ornamentation. The building rose from a limestone base to ornate terra-cotta above. The detailing was designed by Frederick P. Dinkelberg, who worked in Burnham's office.

The Fuller Building went up like a skyrocket. The foundation was completed on March 3, 1902, and exactly four months later the roof was placed in position. On

Pictured here in 1910, the Fuller Building was blamed for damaging winds.

August 1, only nine months after ground was broken, the building was completed.

Rising 300 feet, the Fuller Building was a marvel of architecture, appearing to part the avenues like a great ship. The 23rd Street exposure was a mere 6.5 feet wide, broadening southward to fill the 22nd Street block between Fifth Avenue and Broadway.

The tiny point on the sidewalk level was essentially useless, so Black had a retail space added on that was not on Burnham's original plans. The "cowcatcher" store, Black felt, would take advantage of the busy site and produce income.

Because of its triangular shape, the Fuller Building quickly gained the nickname the "Flatiron Building"—a moniker being tagged on other similarly shaped buildings at the time.

The steel skeleton, said to be the heaviest in New York at 3,680 tons, allowed the structure to attain its full twenty stories plus attic. New Yorkers by now were accustomed to higher and higher buildings. But they were not quite so sure about the effects that the great wedge of masonry would have on air currents.

Because of those concerns the Fuller Building had another nickname: Burnham's Folly.

Upon its completion the *Municipal Journal & Public Works* said, "New York's latest freak in the shape of sky scrapers has already been nicknamed the 'Flat-Iron,' although it is otherwise known as the Fuller Building." Almost immediately rumors began circulating about the building's effects on the wind.

In 1903 the *America Druggist and Pharmaceutical Record* reported that "the erection of this building is said to have had a curious effect in regard to air currents and a case is at present pending in the New York courts, one man suing the owners of the building for a large sum as compensation for the blowing in of his windows, which has happened several times since the building was erected."

The article continued, "Then the street passengers are knocked about in all sorts of rude and unkindly fashions, so that it appears as if the Flat Iron Building may not be an unmixed blessing to the locality."

On February 6, 1903, the *New York Times* blamed increased wind gusts the day before on the Flatiron Building, saying the storm "took up its headquarters in the Flatiron Building. . . . Conservative guessers who drifted past the building during the afternoon estimated the velocity at 1,000 miles an hour. . . . A $500 plate glass window, twelve by eight feet, which adorned the café of the Hotel Bartholdi, directly opposite the Flatiron Building, was the first victim of the wind."

The reporter continued, "Later in the day a recoil gust of wind smashed in one of the three windows of the extension which forms the northern corner of the Flatiron Building."

Fourteen-year-old John McTaggart's death that day was blamed on the building. The messenger boy was attempting to round the 23rd Street point of the building

The building seemed to float up the avenues like a monumental ship.

against the wind. After attempting three times, he was reportedly blown into Fifth Avenue and fatally injured by an automobile.

Then on September 17, 1903, the *Times* reported on another windstorm. "When the storm was at its height, Madison Square for an area of 200 yards from the Flatiron Building was swept clear of all traffic. Anything less heavy than a street car that came within the zone dominated by the triangular structure was blown away."

A concerned citizen from Newport, Rhode Island, J. A. Swan wrote to the newspaper suggesting a solution. "In regard to the trouble at the Flatiron Building, which we read about every time we have a high wind, has it been suggested by anybody that it could be all remedied, without spoiling the looks of the building, by putting a balcony about four feet wide around the building just below the windows at every story, or every other story? I have been convinced in my own mind from the first that this would prevent the wind from sweeping down after it strikes the building."

Not everyone was concerned about the wind's effects. Policemen were kept busy shooing away the young men who loitered at the 23rd Street point of the building, hoping an errant gust of wind would lift the hems of passing ladies, exposing a tantalizing glimpse of ankle.

Wind worries eventually subsided and in March 1905 plans were filed with the Building Department to increase the height of the skyscraper. A "draughting

The façade is
encrusted with
Intricate carving,
much of it unseen
from street level.

room" was charted as an additional story "ten feet high with several skylights." The estimated cost of the addition, which would bring the building to a full 22 stories, was $10,000.

Four years later the effectiveness of the water pressure in the soaring building—thoroughly tested in 1902—would be put to the test again when a fire raged on the 21st floor. Firefighters were required to wrestle high-pressure hoses from the lower floors up the stairs in a five-hour battle with the flames.

The Flatiron looms peacefully in the background as carriages and pedestrians make their way along Fifth Avenue after a snowstorm.

Although the structure was little damaged, the heat did dislodge one of the large ornamental blocks—about four feet wide and a foot thick—from the façade. The block fell twenty-one floors to Fifth Avenue, missing a policeman by a few feet. The concussion of the masonry onto the pavement broke a plate-glass window in the Stein Doblin Company at Broadway and 22nd Street.

Throughout its existence the Flatiron Building has remained an icon of New York City. In their *Beaux-Arts Architecture in New York*, Edmund Vincent Gillon, Jr., and Henry Hope Reed wrote, "Of all the skyscrapers built in the first decades of this century, the Flatiron Building was the one that captured the public imagination— even more than did the Woolworth Building."

It has been the focus of esteemed photographers such as Berenice Abbott, Alfred Stieglitz, and Edward Steichen; the subject of paintings by Albert Gleizes, Paul Cornoyer, and other American artists; appeared in the writings of O. Henry and scores of television shows and motion pictures. Even before its completion the Flatiron Building was one of the most recognizable and most reproduced architectural images in the United States.

The beloved Flatiron Building has given its name to the entire geographical area around it: the Flatiron District. And today it still functions as an office building, housing some of the nation's most renowned publishing companies.

REFINED REMNANTS

178–180 FIFTH AVENUE

Even as New York's boys marched south to fight in the war of rebellion, Fifth Avenue below 23rd Street continued developing as the city's most exclusive residential thoroughfare. In 1862 C. A. Pepoon erected three brownstone mansions at Nos. 176 to 180, meant to appear as a single grand home.

Italianate in style, the combined homes were reminiscent of a smart English townhouse. The central house at No. 178 projected slightly from its flanking neighbors and its pedimented cornice was mimicked in the treatment of the third-floor windows. The more subdued houses at Nos. 176 and 180 carried out the unified design.

Business was quick to push the city's millionaires north and only ten years after the houses were built, No. 178 had already fallen to commerce. In 1872, Margaret S. Fischer paid the staggering amount of $59 a square foot for No. 178—about $1,000 in today's dollars. The *New York Times* later mused that "its proximity to Madison Square probably accounted in large measure for the high price of this parcel."

Fischer removed the stoops, installed vast bayed shop windows at the parlor level, and storefronts on the first floor. The third and fourth floors were leased as apartments.

The upper floors of No. 180 would be the scene of scandalous and tragic publicity in 1875. Thomas B. Whitney, the son of Thomas B. Whitney, a well-known brewer, was wealthy in his own right. The *Times* said that he "owns a large interest in the brewery and other business concerns and is possessed of a considerable yearly income."

Young Whitney was also a frequent client of brothels. When he returned from Europe in 1874, he went to one of his favorite establishments several times where he purchased the favors of "an inmate of which he had a previous acquaintance," according to the newspaper. But on one visit he noticed another girl, Elizabeth Roane, who went by the name of Minge.

Minge was 20 years old, "a brunette, well educated, and of very handsome appearance," according to the *Times*. She had her own servant girl, named Euphemia Baptiste. The 25-year-old Whitney was swept away by the young girl. The *Times* said, "Whitney fell in love with her, and she with him, as far as such women can be supposed to love."

It was beyond social possibility that the two could marry, but Whitney proposed that she become his mistress and she accepted. "He at once hired a flat in the brownstone house No. 180 Fifth Avenue, and furnished it in sumptuous style, sparing no expense or trouble in securing the most costly and unique articles of furniture."

Two additional servants were hired and the pair moved in during February of 1875. Although they were happy together, Minge was jealous of the girls Whitney had formerly patronized. On November 9 that year when Whitney came home Minge brought

Only the center and northern homes survive of the original harmonious trio.

up the name of a particular prostitute. He attempted to ignore the subject.

He later testified that "we sat down to dinner about 6:30 o'clock; she treated me rather coldly, but did not say one angry word; at dinner we each drank three or four glasses of ale, as was our usual custom; after she wanted some chestnuts, and I sent the colored servant girl out for some, and laid down on the sofa and went to sleep."

Minge woke him up accusing him, "Tom, you don't care for me anymore." Whitney refused to discuss the subject and went back to sleep on the bed. She woke him up again saying, "Tom, if you don't get up and talk to me you will regret it forever."

Again Tom told her to leave him alone and let him sleep.

He was awakened by the report of his pistol. He found Minge lying on the sofa with a bullet hole through her heart. The girl had purposely staged her death so that Whitney would "regret it forever."

Investigators questioned the doctor who arrived at the scene. A reporter from *The New York Times* recounted his story: "She took from her wardrobe and put on a silk wrapper which Whitney had brought from Turkey, and attired in which, he had often informed her, she appeared to most advantage. She then dressed her hair in a fashion most admired by her lover, and lying down on the lounge, shot herself."

Thomas Whitney was overcome with grief. The *New York Times* reported, "By order of Whitney, the body of the unfortunate young girl was placed in a magnificent rosewood casket, mounted in solid silver, and having on the plate this inscription: 'Minge Roane, died Nov. 9, 1875, aged twenty-one years.'"

Although the funeral was nearly private—held in an undertaker's establishment on Sixth Avenue—the hall was filled with flowers. "Around the room were arranged so many floral tributes, columns, crosses, cushions, anchors, etc., that when they were taken away they filled three carriages."

Minge's many friends, presumably from the brothels, were refused entrance to the service. "Only Mr. Whitney's friends were admitted to the rooms where the corpse lay," said the *Times*. "In the afternoon the street was lined with curious lookers-on, among whom many were evidently mourners, who had drawn up in elegant coaches, and whose dress indicated luxury and extravagance."

In 1879 the store at No. 180 became home to F. W. Christern, booksellers. Christern catered to the educated, upper middle class. Next door was another bookstore, G.P. Putnam's Sons.

The same year that Christern opened his store here, Colonel Henry C. Logan moved to New York from California. At 18 years old, in 1848, Logan had left Baltimore for the West. The *New York Times* would later say, "His career there was daring and successful." He gained his title in the California militia and organized the San Francisco Stock Exchange, serving as its president for a time. Now in New York, he joined the banking and brokerage firm of Prince & Whitely and took rooms at No. 180.

Unlike other successful financiers of the time, Logan did not amass great wealth. He preferred to see others less fortunate make use of his money. The *Times* said, "Although some of Col. Logan's operations were large, he was too generous to accumulate much of a fortune. Any needy Californian could always command his purse."

On the evening of April 14, 1887, he suffered dizziness in his rooms here. As he fell, he struck his left temple against a desk. Colonel Logan never regained consciousness and died on April 15.

Christern's bookstore moved northward, to be replaced by Dunlap & Co, Hatters in Nos. 178 and 180. The 1891 *History and Commerce of New York* described the store: "Here [Robert Dunlap] occupies two floors, 50 x 100 feet each, one devoted to the wholesale and one to the retail department.... Every hat bearing the Dunlap trade mark is a gem of art and taste, and so well understood is this fact that the resources of the house are taxed, after meeting its enormous city patronage, to supply the demands at wholesale, for the Dunlap hats are typical in every city in the Union."

The same year *King's Handbook of the United States* said, "The crown and culmination of a gentleman's apparel is his hat; and the originator and leader of styles in this country is the firm of R. Dunlap & Co., whose main retail store is at 178–180 Fifth Avenue." Robert Dunlap had founded the business in 1857 and remained its only principal.

On March 9, 1895, Madison Square Garden opened its International Costume Exhibition. Both modern and historical costumes were presented and New York society filed in to the gala event. The following day the *New York Times* reported that "The exhibition made by R. Dunlap & Co. of 178 and 180 Fifth Avenue, comprises head gear worn by eminent women from the Fifteenth century to the early part of the Nineteenth, and also the latest novelties for the present season. Most conspicuous among the number are the duplicates of hats worn by Queen Elizabeth and Marie Antoinette. The Dutch hat, which is so popular now, is shown as it was worn in Holland during the Seventeenth century." The newspaper added, "The firm has endeavored to have this display absolutely correct in every detail."

In 1896 merchant tailor Charles H. Maguire was living in No. 178 and running his business on the second floor. A 55-year-old bachelor, he suffered two strokes in August, the first at the Brighton Beach race track, and a second at the Norwegian Hospital in Brooklyn. The second stroke proved fatal.

Officials placed a personal ad in the morning newspapers requesting Maguire's sister, Mrs. Henrietta Mead, to contact the hospital. The ad stated the tailor had "left considerable property and some jewelry" at the facility.

At the turn of the century parts of the upper floors were leased to small commercial tenants. In 1910 Herman Lee Meader not only lived in No. 178 but also operated his architectural office here. The following year he would draft the plans for a 24-story hotel at the northeast corner of Seventh Avenue and 37th Street. He told reporters that in his estimation it would be the tallest hotel not only in New York, but in the world. Sadly for Meader, the ambitious building was never constructed.

Gerry Cathcart, a paint manufacturer, paid a visit to the apartment of John Scott Anderson in No. 180 in July 1911. Anderson was an insurance manager with an office at No. 149 Broadway and was married to the former Agnes Ritchie. The pair had three daughters—Louise, Beatrice, and Nancy. Cathcart was surprised when the door to the apartment was opened.

He found himself testifying before Referee Phoenix Ingraham in court on March 19, 1912. "Cathcart said he had known Anderson for thirty years. He also knew Mrs. Anderson. On the occasion of his July visit to the apartment, Cathcart said he saw a woman who was not Mrs. Anderson. Cathcart's companion, Thomas W. Heffron,

In the 1920s the block still showed its residential roots. All three houses survive, altered, at Nos. 176–180 in the middle of the block.

also testified to seeing a woman attired 'in just a little fancy gauze work' in the Anderson apartment," relayed the *New York Times*.

Agnes Ritchie Anderson received a decree of absolute divorce, $125 a month alimony, and custody of the girls.

In 1920, Dunlap & Co. moved to 431 Fifth Avenue. Retlau Trading Company took the store and basement of No. 178, and Emmanuel & Anthony De Mos took the store and basement in No. 180 where "the lessees will open a confectionery and lunchroom," said the newspapers.

The buildings continued to see the coming and going of various businesses. In 1922 Purvin Typewriter took an entire floor of No. 178. A year later United Shoe Rebuilding Corporation moved in to the street-level store.

In 1927 what was still a beautiful trio of buildings lost its symmetry when No. 176 was demolished by the Connell Holding Co. to erect a modern store and loft building. In 1939 the surviving pair were converted to apartments above the sidewalk level. In 1943 Arrowhead Press was in the building and that year released the war-song book *Give Out—Songs Of, By and For the Men in Service*.

In 1936 80-year old artist and illustrator Reginald Bathurst Birch leased a studio on the top floor of No. 178. That year he completed work on illustrations for Frank

Stockton's *The Reformed Pirate* and some for Ogden Nash's *A Bad Parent's Garden of Verses*. But Birch would forever be best remembered for the illustrations of *Little Lord Fauntleroy* he had produced 40 years earlier.

The feisty octogenarian refused to believe his true age until Lincoln Barnett of the *New York Times* did the arithmetic. On May 3 that year Barnett wrote "It took a pencil and paper and quite a little persuasion to convince him, for the white-haired handsome little man…kept pounding the table and insisting he was seventy-nine."

When Birch calmed down a bit and accepted his true age, he talked about his lifestyle and his studio. "At eighty he makes no effort to limit his nicotine, he walks up five flights of stairs to reach his studio; he believes that 'after a certain age a certain amount of whisky is good for any man,'" said Barnett.

"He stints himself only in food and the matter of living quarters. 'Of course I don't like this garret,' he said. 'In fact I object to it very strongly. But I can't move because I owe my landlord money.'"

Among the tenants upstairs in No. 178 were Miriam Hecht and her husband. She wrote to the editor of the *New York Times* in 1991 remembering the space where they lived from the late 1940s until January 1957.

"Our studio apartment two flights above street level, probably a converted master bedroom, featured a 13-foot ceiling ornamented with plaster festoons, a huge marble fireplace in working order, 9-foot windows, and an enormous bathtub."

Today the careworn façades of the two remaining houses retain the 1872 shop windows installed by Margaret Fischer. Above, they still look amazingly house-like—the last vestiges of a time when this block of Fifth Avenue was New York's finest neighborhood.

CHELSEA

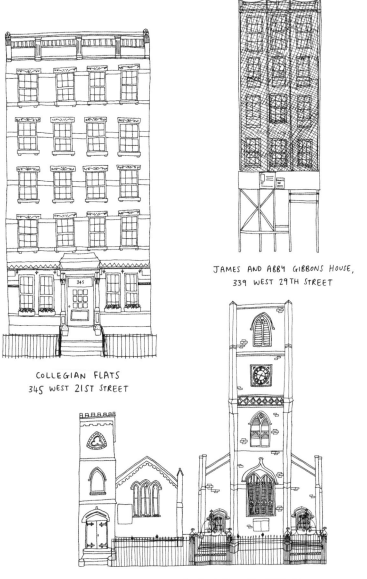

JAMES AND ABBY GIBBONS HOUSE,
339 WEST 29TH STREET

COLLEGIAN FLATS
345 WEST 21ST STREET

ST PETER'S CHURCH   WEST 20TH STREET

ST. PETER'S EPISCOPAL CHURCH

WEST 20TH STREET

In an impressive act of forward thinking, the Commissioners Plan of 1811 laid out the streets and avenues of Manhattan above 14th Street in a logical, geometrical scheme far superior to the rambling, twisted roadways of the lower island. On paper, the Plan dissected the sprawling country estates of New York's wealthy landowners that occupied what would become Midtown and Uptown Manhattan.

Among these was Chelsea, the family estate of Clement Clarke Moore. A century later it would not be Moore's esteemed standing in the community, his philanthropies, nor his real estate development for which he would be remembered. Instead it was the Christmas poem he wrote in 1823, "A Visit from St. Nicholas," or "The Night Before Christmas," that immortalized him. Moore's estate was named after Chelsea Old Church in London of which his grandfather, Thomas Clarke, a British army officer, had been a member before settling in America in 1750.

Seven years after the publication of the Commissioners' Plan, Moore donated 66 tracts of land—a full city block—for the establishment of the General Theological Seminary of the Episcopal Church. The first building on what would become known as Chelsea Square was completed in 1826. The growing seminary fostered a rapidly expanding community, as brick and brownstone residences began cropping up on lots sold by Moore.

Within five years a chapel was deemed necessary, and seven lots of land were leased from Moore for the purpose, just a half block away on 20th Street.

The chapel was planned in the summer of 1831 with the Rev. Benjamin I. Haight from the seminary serving, according to Jonathan Greenleaf in 1846, as "a slated supply." Clement Clarke Moore was highly instrumental in the design of the chapel, insisting on the Greek Revival style. It was a preference that was to be expected in a time when Christian churches mainly took the form of classical temples, often sporting columned porticoes.

The brown brick structure, a bit box-like, opened on February 4, 1832. That year *The Banner of the Church* noted "The building...is intended to accommodate

The fieldstone tower rises regally above 20th Street.

the congregation until the vestry shall have in it the power to erect a large and commodious church."

The Chelsea neighborhood was still largely rural and undeveloped, and the tiny congregation consisted of only twenty-two members. Historian Jonathan Greenleaf, in his 1846 *A History of the Churches, of All Denominations, in the City of New York*, wrote "Mr. Haight continued as the supply until December 1, 1833, when he was duly instituted as Rector. In the next year he resigned this charge, and removed to Cincinnati."

Haight was replaced on November 2, 1834 by the English-born Rev. Thomas Pyne. Pyne's liberal views regarding human rights, however, would soon get him into hot water. According to historian Christopher Edwards in his notes on *Canons for the Government of the Protestant Episcopal Church in the United States of America*, "he was dismissed in 1835 for preaching a Thanksgiving Sermon advocating the emancipation of slaves." The fact that Clement Clarke Moore, who was highly involved in the church, was an ardent anti-abolitionist no doubt hastened Pyne's abrupt departure.

Shortly after Pyne returned to England the Rev. Hugh Smith took over as rector of St. Peter's. By now, development in the neighborhood was booming and the congregation had greatly outgrown the little Greek Revival chapel. Smith initiated a new building project on the lot next door to the chapel—an impressive gray stone church in the English Gothic style. The new St. Peter's Church would be one of the first Gothic-style houses of worship in Manhattan.

Built by James W. Smith, the handsome church was dedicated on February 22, 1838, and the former chapel was converted into the parsonage house—an extremely early example of structural recycling. Dominating the new building was the soaring square bell tower, visible for blocks away. A massive stained-glass window in the tower base flooded the interior with light. The entrance sat far back from the sidewalk above broad stone steps that created a wide plaza.

At the time, surrounding Trinity Church in downtown Manhattan, stood a post-colonial-period fence erected between 1788 and 1790. The church building, dating from 1788, suffered severe structural weakness brought on by the heavy snows of the winter of 1838–39. The old church building was razed and a new one begun; the 18th-century fencing and gate were given as a gift to the new St. Peter's Church.

Clement Clarke Moore remained an integral part of the St. Peter's parish. He was an early warden and vestryman and donated the excellent organ. And he sometimes played it, as well. In 1904 an elderly parishioner recalled in a letter to the *New York Times* Moore's playing in 1841 when the writer was a child: "He was a fine organist, and sometimes used to play on this organ, though he was quite an old man, as I remember him, which I do perfectly well."

The writer reminisced about the no-frills Episcopal approach to religion in those days. "There were no 'Sunday school festivals' nor Christmas trees. The only thing in that line for the holidays was on New Year's Day, when the children all assembled in the body of the church and our rector addressed them, and as they afterward marched in line past him in the chancel he handed each one a New Year's cake, which he took from two large clothes baskets on each side of him, wishing us a Happy New Year at the same time."

In 1853 the parish was building again; this time on the lot to the east of the church. To the rear of the lot a schoolhouse was constructed and completed that same year. In 1854, within a few months of the new building's opening, Rev. Dr. Alfred B. Beach took the pulpit of St. Peter's. Along with the spiritual needs of his congregation, he took on its financial problems as well.

All the construction had come with a price and St. Peter's was, unfortunately, unable to meet the costs. A year after the school was completed, Beach applied to Trinity Church for aid to cover its staggering $30,000 debts. Trinity agreed to lend the church $25,000 on the condition that Clement Clarke Moore donate the land, still being leased, to the church. He agreed.

Two years later, St. Peter's knocked on the door of Trinity Church once again asking for financial aid. This time Trinity refused. However, under Dr. Alfred Beach's capable management, St. Peter's Church struggled on and survived.

The church attracted a near mob when the funeral of a murdered man named Walton took place here on July 3, 1860. Details of the crime involved the "peculiar domestic relations of Mr. and Mrs. Walton," quarreling among the extended family, and a sordid scandal. It was the type of sensationalism that Victorians openly abhorred and privately relished. The funeral, reported the *New York Times*, "attracted a large crowd."

Despite its liturgical similarities with the Roman Catholic Church, the Episcopal Church consistently made clear the differences between its beliefs and those of "the Papists." In 1870 the First Vatican Council pronounced a series of new tenets, including the infallibility of the Pope. The Rev. Dr. Beach wasted no time in spouting his opinions from the pulpit of St. Peter's on March 20. Using St. Paul's assertion to "Prove all things; hold fast that which is good," he diplomatically cautioned the congregation not to simply scoff at the concept—since thousands of Catholics would accept it—but to follow Paul's advice. The clergyman's diplomacy was thinly veiled. "The reverend gentleman said that however unreasonable and absurd any claim made on their religious faith may be, they could hardly be justified in treating it with contempt so long as they knew there was a considerable number of their fellow-beings who, through ignorance or otherwise, were entertaining it seriously," reported the *New York Times.*

In 1873 the parish built what Floyd Appleton in *Church Philanthropy in New York* called "a fine Gothic Hall" in front of the school building. Now the wide swath of property appeared to be a collection of three charming churches, each distinctively different and all aligned in a picturesque grouping.

Dr. Beach suffered a stroke in 1890, ending his pastorate of thirty-six years. Following his death in 1897 the congregation collected donations from parishioners and friends. In tribute to his service, on October 7, 1900 and after a considerable period of construction, the new altar, a reredos, a processional painting, and a monumental stained-glass memorial window were unveiled. The window, *The Calling of St. Peter*, was designed by Frederick S. Lamb and executed by J. and R. Lamb. Its installation required that part of a wall be removed.

Meanwhile Chelsea continued to grow and change. As the neighborhood developed areas of poverty and crime near the waterfront contrasted with dignified brownstone and brick homes along the side streets nearer Eighth Avenue. In 1902, Rufus Rockwell Wilson, in his *New York: Old & New,* commented on the surviving quaintness of the church: "Old Chelsea families are still represented in the vestry, and the scholarly repose of Chelsea Square on the opposite side of the way preserves in its surroundings something of the quiet which rested upon them before Chelsea became a part of the city."

"THE CALLING OF ST. PETER."

Chas window erected in St. Peter's Church, West Twentieth-st., New-York City. Designed by
Frederick S. Lamb and executed by J. and R. Lamb.

On October 7, 1900 the *New-York Tribune* published a photograph of the new window.

In 1919, *Valentine's Manual of Old New York* noted that, "The records of this old church deserve a chapter by themselves, for they contain the marriages, births and deaths of many of the best known families in this city. It may no longer rank as one of the fashionable churches, but it remains one of the oldest and most interesting."

In December 1936, as St. Peter's Church began plans for its upcoming centennial, a gift arrived from England. At the annual memorial service for Clement Clarke Moore a stone from the tower of Chelsea Old Church was presented.

On February 22, 1938, the centennial was celebrated. A letter was read from the church's oldest parishioner, Miss Annie Emery, one of the original congregants. Born on November 27, 1836, she was a year and a half old when the church was consecrated. Miss Emery understandably decided on a congratulatory letter "since she believes her strength will not permit her to be present at the service," said the *Times.*

Another letter came from President Franklin D. Roosevelt who wrote in part, "I trust that many a year to come the rich spiritual life which for so long has emanated from this century-old foundation may continue an ever extending influence for good in Chelsea and the entire community."

Roosevelt's assumption proved true. Today, St. Peter's Church remains an important institution in the Chelsea community, although the makeup of its parishioners is somewhat different than in 1838. The Gothic Hall has been converted to an off-Broadway theater by the Atlantic Theater Company; but the parsonage and gray fieldstone church remain untouched.

And around it all, the iron fence, two centuries old, still stands. Meyer Berger in his 2004 book *Meyer Berger's New York* mused, "Puerto Rican children play around the old St. Peter's Gate now and probably don't know that a long time ago the old gate had swung to the touch of George Washington, Alexander Hamilton, Robert Fulton and Capt. James Lawrence. It shows no sign of wear."

MURDER IN THE COLLEGIAN FLATS

345 WEST 21ST STREET

By 1884 the quiet and respectable block of West 21st Street between Eighth and Ninth Avenues was undergoing change. Its brick and brownstone one-family homes were slowly being converted into boarding houses. And before the end of the century several of them would be razed to make way for modern apartment buildings.

One of the very first of these was built by the Simon Estate at No. 345 and would be, as the *New York Times* put it, "dignified by the title of the Collegian Flats." Built for middle-class families, the five-story building offered two roomy apartments per floor, with tall double-hung windows for ample ventilation.

The red-brick building was trimmed in stone with up-to-the-minute Eastlake touches—a saw-tooth cornice between the first and second floors, for instance, and incised lintel carvings. The rows of windows at each level were connected by a stone course at the sills and at the lintels, and by a decorative floral tile band—a nice added touch. Two semi-attached polished granite columns supported a solid stone hood over the entrance, proclaiming that this was not another tenement building.

The Collegian Flats would quickly become the center of a scandalous murder trial that started far away in Cleveland, Ohio.

In May 1884, 24-year-old George W. Evans stopped at the American Hotel in Cleveland. Across the street was the Johnson House where Annie Beltz, "a very attractive young woman," according to newspapers, was a guest. Annie was the daughter of a Steubenville livery stable owner and had argued with her parents and run away from home.

Evans flirted with Annie through the hotel windows, finally becoming acquainted with her. What Annie did not know was that he was the son of Alexander Evans, a notorious pickpocket and sneak thief also known as "Nevins," and "the milkman." Nor did she know he was cruel and abusive.

Evans was attracted to the young girl not only for her good looks, but also for the $40,000 of Steubenville property of which she would someday become the sole heiress. He convinced Annie to come back to New York with him and in the fall they were married. On November 1 he was hired as janitor of the new Collegian Flats. The couple was given the four-room apartment in the basement. Things seemed to be going well for the newlyweds.

Trouble soon surfaced. The jealous husband felt that Augustus White, a partner in the management company of the building, W. A. White & Sons, was taking too great an interest in his wife and that she appeared to reciprocate. Quarrels ensued.

Tenants began complaining that Evans would lock himself in the apartment with his wife and beat her. According to the *New York Times*, "sounds of blows and shrieks indicated that he was chastising her, and she afterward complained that he not only beat her, but tried to strangle her." The residents were, reported the *Times*: "shocked by Evans's brutality to his wife."

The *Sun* was less sympathetic. It reported that the tenants "suggested to the agents that he should be removed from the flats, as the woman's cries were annoying."

By January, Annie Evans was fearful for her life. When White called one morning and Evans was not at home, she implored the man to help her.

"She said she had discovered that her husband, whom she married hastily, was a villain," White later recounted. "He had a bad temper and had beaten her and threatened to kill her. She told me she was afraid for her life and begged me to help her to get back to her home and friends in Ohio. Unless I did so she would be driven to kill herself."

A plan was hatched whereby Annie would have enough time to pack and escape. On Wednesday, January 28, Evans was summoned to the White offices at 1:00 p.m. to discuss maintenance of the water pipes in the building. When he arrived, White told him he had to take care of something, but not to leave until he returned.

White finally came back at six in the evening, apologized and asked Evans to return the next day. When the janitor arrived at the basement apartment, he found that his wife had packed and left. In the morning he was fired and told to leave.

George Evans, however, did not take losing his wife or losing his job easily. He spent twenty-four hours searching for Annie and at one point was informed she had been seen "walking with Mr. White." Evans was enraged.

When he returned to the apartment on Friday at 11:30 p.m., he encountered the new janitor, a black man named Thomas Currie. The two got into a violent argument, which was heard on the uppermost floor. Edmund Coon's apartment on the top floor connected to the coal bins in the cellar by a shaft descending from the rear room. Thomas Coon, a nephew, was awakened by the angry voices below.

"I want you to understand I'm janitor here until tomorrow; then my time's up. I have orders not to let anyone in the house at night. So you get."

The 36-year-old Currie argued that he was obeying the orders of White to stay.

Edmund Coon, who was in the front room of the apartment at the time, was startled by a gunshot. His nephew told him what he had heard and the pair listened

The apartment building exhibited the latest in architectural style.

at the shaft, first hearing groaning, then, "What did you expect—that I'd let you 'boss' me? I had to defend myself. Do you want a doctor?"

The men rushed to the basement to find a dazed Currie at the foot of the cellar stairs, bleeding from the head. He was able to say that Evans had shot him. He was taken to New York Hospital where he died four days later.

The manhunt was on for Evans whom police described as "5 feet 9 inches in height, small side whiskers, small black mustache, black hair and eyes, ruddy complexion, medium build, dark clothes and a derby hat."

Assuming that Annie fled to Ohio, Evans headed there. Authorities tracked him to Cleveland, Chicago, and St. Louis; and then lost the trail. Nearly a year would pass before Evans was caught. Detectives rented a room across the street from Evans's aunt who lived at 312 East 105th Street on a hunch that he might return to New York. Finally, in December, they spotted him at the window of his aunt's apartment.

He was arrested later on the street. In the waistband of his trousers was a pearl-handled double-edged dagger 7 inches long. Evans confessed to the killing.

But it would not be the end of the story.

On January 21, 1886, George W. Evans appeared in court to face his first-degree murder charge. The *Times* sized him up for its readers. "As he sat in the Court of Oyer and Terminer yesterday, on trial for murder in the first degree, he looked very different from the typical criminal. He had a clean-cut face, a clear complexion, and a bright, intelligent expression. By his attire he showed himself possessed of good taste. But there was a flippancy about him that was not pleasant to see in the manner of a man on trial for murder."

When Evans's attorney, William F. Howe, stood before the jury, the account of the killing was drastically changed. According to Howe's version, Evans had acted solely in self-defense. The counsel insisted that when Currie was told to leave, he refused and drew a revolver. Evans then pulled out his own gun and Currie relented, putting his in the pocket of his overcoat. When Evans turned to leave to summon a policeman to oust the intruder, Currie said "Now I'll kill you."

But Evans was faster than Currie, recounted Howe, and his bullet stopped the would-be murderer. When Evans realized that the new janitor was shot, he fled because he did not have enough money to hire an attorney to defend himself.

Two days later, a verdict was reached. Evans was guilty of manslaughter in the first degree, punishable by fifteen years in prison. "He took the verdict of the jury and his sentence coolly," said the *Times*, "and without evident emotion, nor did he break down or show either the quivering of the lip or the moistening of an eyelid when his father, mother, and grandmother gave vent to their feelings in great sobs of grief."

Evans's attorney had more tricks up his sleeve, however.

When Thomas Currie had identified Evans as the shooter, detectives were required to ask the question "Have you any hope of recovering from the effects of the injury you have received?" The question was necessary to establish an "*ante-mortem* statement," one made by a person believing he was about to die.

Currie replied, "It is hard for me to say."

William F. Howe appealed to the Supreme Court. If Currie was not certain that he was going to die, his statement could not be "*ante-mortem*." Evans was granted a new trial.

In a plot twist that is inconceivable today, the General Term of the Supreme Court set aside the verdict on June 1, 1886, on the grounds that the dying man's statement was not "a legal *ante-mortem* statement." There was no retrial because, as reported in the *New York Times*, "the only evidence against him beyond the excluded statement of Currie is circumstantial and not strong."

George Evans, the cruel and malicious physical abuser of his young wife and the cold-blooded murderer of Thomas Currie, was a free man.

The Collegian Flats never again was the subject of such dark publicity. Reputable tenants continued to live here, for example Susanne Pallett, who was here in 1911. A member of the Daughters of the American Revolution, she was descended from John Hart who served under Captain John Prout Sloan on the Marine sloop *Enterprise* in 1775.

There was, however, a bit of embarrassment when resident and truck driver William P. Jones was arrested for his involvement with a band of pier thieves. John Quinn was employed as a checker by the Lehigh Valley Railroad at Pier 30. Quinn would steal valuable freight, such as silverware, that was transported by Jones to others who would sell the goods.

But for the most part, the lives of residents at 345 West 21st Street such as Lt. Francis E. Liszanckie of Fire Engine Company 8 who lived here in 1951, were quiet and unexceptional.

In 1974 the building was converted from two to four apartments per floor. Otherwise, the prim and attractive Victorian apartment building is unchanged. Its Chelsea residents come and go unaware that in the 1880s its basement was the scene of one of the most publicized murders in New York.

JAMES AND ABBY GIBBONS HOUSE

339 WEST 29TH STREET

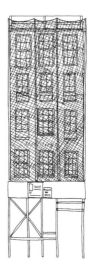

As the eighteenth century turned into the nineteenth, the bucolic landscape above 14th Street was still dotted with the country estates of New York's gentry. It was a noble lifestyle that would not last much longer. In 1811 the Commissioners' Plan divided the upper portion of the island into a regimented grid of avenues and streets that would end forever the era of Manhattan's rural mansions.

Cornelius Ray was a latecomer, purchasing land just to the north of Clement Clarke Moore's family estate, Chelsea, in the early years of the 1800s. Ray's property stretched from the Hudson River to what is approximately now Eighth Avenue, from about 27th Street to 30th Street. By the time he died in 1827, construction had already begun along Eighth Avenue to the south. Five years later his children began dividing the estate into building lots.

Among the developers who would change the face of the Chelsea neighborhood were Cyrus Mason and William Torrey. Most notably they constructed the elegant upscale London Terrace on West 23rd Street in 1845—a block-long row of homes set back from the street by green lawns. A two-story colonnade ran the length of the row, which pretended to be a single magnificent building.

A year after the completion of London Terrace, the men turned their attention to the block between Eighth and Ninth Avenues on 29th Street. They purchased the northern block front from the Ray Estate and obtained the rights to the lots on the opposite side of the street. To make their tiny new residences more marketable, a park was developed on the south side to increase sunlight, ventilation, and attractive views. They renamed the block Lamartine Place (the park was called Lamartine Park) to add to the exclusive tone.

Construction turned out to be a slow process. The final homes were not completed until 1852. But the finished project was exactly what the developers intended: a row of distinguished residences set behind small lawns with iron fences. The three-story Greek Revival–style homes drew upper-middle-class buyers.

While Mason and Torrey were busy developing Chelsea, a Quaker couple was working with those in need. James Sloan Gibbons had married Abigail Hopper in

Veiled in construction netting for years, the historic house suffers neglect and disrepair.

1833 in Philadelphia. Upon moving to New York two years later, Abby established a school for black children in her home while her banker husband worked for the Bank of the State of New York. Gibbons would later publish several books on banking. But it was not finance for which he would be remembered.

The Quaker couple diligently worked for those in need. In addition to the little school she ran from her home, Abby organized the German Industrial School to help homeless immigrant children and the New York Infant Asylum for unwed mothers and orphans. She made weekly visits to the Tombs prison downtown, concerned with the welfare of the children held here. Lydia Maria Child in her *Letters from New York*, told of James Gibbons frequently visiting the squalid and dangerous Five Points neighborhood "with a basket containing food, medicine, clothing, etc., which he would distribute to the poor."

In 1851 the Gibbons couple purchased No. 17 Lamartine Place. Abby Gibbons outfitted the house with new purchases and then was concerned that her father, the social reformer Isaac Hopper, would disapprove of her over-spending. She would later write to a friend that her father overlooked the stairway carpeting, but criticized the plush parlor rug as "extravagant."

Isaac Hopper caught a cold in December of that year while traveling to visit a discharged prisoner. A month later his condition had deteriorated and in March 1852 the Gibbons family took him into the Lamartine Place house to tend to him. Despite the loving care, he died in the house in May of that year.

Within a few months Abby and James purchased the house next door at No. 19 and moved their family from the house where Isaac Hopper died. Abby continued her work with underprivileged children. She was well known for her Christmas dolls that were distributed to children in prisons and the Almshouse. Two days before Christmas in 1856 the *New York Times* reported that, "Once a year about forty ladies of this City, whose benevolence is directed by a correct appreciation of the desires of little folks, meet together and prepare for presentation to the children under the care of the Governors of the Almshouse, a large number of those child's delights, know as doll-babies." The newspaper noted that "such a presentation has been made every Christmas day for a number of years" and the group of women had met the prior evening in the house of Abby Gibbons.

Here, the article said, "they dressed some six or seven hundred dolls, that otherwise would, in all probability, have remained stark naked during the most inclement season of the year." Abby and her group convinced local merchants to donate remnants of ribbons, material, and "fancy goods" from which they made the doll clothes.

Like Isaac Hopper, the Gibbons's were staunchly anti-slavery. James Gibbons supported the *Anti-Slavery Standard*, an Abolitionist newspaper. In a city whose merchants greatly supported the institution of slavery, the family daringly and rather openly made the house on Lamartine Place a stop in the Underground Railroad. Slaves escaping to Canada were welcomed in the Gibbons home and given meals, shelter, and whatever aid they needed.

Even among Abolitionists, the Quaker family was unusually democratic in its racial views. A letter written by Joseph Choate mentioned that, "The house of Mrs. Gibbons was a great resort of abolitionists and extreme antislavery people from all parts of the land, as it was one of the stations of the underground railroad by which fugitive slaves found their way from the South to Canada. I have dined with that family in company with William Lloyd Garrison, and sitting at the table with us was a jet-black negro who was on his way to freedom."

When President Abraham Lincoln issued the Emancipation Proclamation in January 1863, James Gibbons "illuminated his house in honor of the proclamation," according to the *Friends' Intelligencer.* The Gibbons daughters hung bunting from the upper windows. It was a bold, in-your-face pronouncement of the Gibbons stance, and it would have severe consequences.

On July 11, 1863, the nation's first attempt at a military draft played out in New York with a lottery. When the 1,200 chosen names were published, it was obvious that only the city's poor and immigrant population was included—the wealthy had obviously bought or used their political power to circumvent the draft. The result was the Draft Riots—a four-day reign of terror and carnage unlike anything seen in the country before.

Draft offices, newspaper buildings, and the homes and neighborhoods of black citizens were burned and looted. The Colored Orphan Asylum was burned to the ground. The black neighborhood of Thompson Street was a target and the *New York Times* reported on "a band of men and boys who were engaged in gathering straw, old barrels, and other combustible materials, for the purpose of kindling a fire among the tenement houses of the negroes."

On the second day of the insurrection the mob moved towards the Gibbons house. At 28th Street and Seventh Avenue they came upon a black man. The *Times* reported that "he was attacked in the street, brutally beaten, his throat cut, and when entirely dead, his body was hung on the nearest lamp-post. It remained suspended there for some hours, until finally a few policemen, who dared to brave the fury of the mob, cut it down and conveyed it to the Station-house."

The rabble proceeded to No. 19 Lamartine Place. Only James and two daughters, Julia and Lucy, were at home. The girls had already begun to move belongings from their home across the roofs to their uncle's nearby house. They watched from an upstairs window of their relatives' home as the crowd mobbed onto Lamartine Place, intent on their house.

The door to the Gibbons house was broken down and the rabble flooded in, ransacking the residence. Family friend Joseph Choate took his life into his hands by entering the house as one of the mob in search of the family. When he found them in the nearby house, he got a carriage and had it wait around the corner. He returned to take the girls across the rooftops to the house of Henry and Esther Herrman where they silently descended to the street. The carriage took them to the safety of the Choate house on West 21st Street where they would stay for several days.

At 5:30 the police arrived. David M. Barnes recorded the moment two months later, writing, "A mob was sacking the residence of Mr. J. S. Gibbons, No. 19 Lamartine Place. The force came upon the rioters, strewing the way with bodies as they went. A large number of rioters and thieves were inside of the building, and while a portion of the command went in, others remained at the front, to receive with the locusts the villains driven out."

At this point the military arrived and, confused by the tangle of police and rioters, fired recklessly and without orders into the crowd. Barnes would report that they injured "more friends than foes." He told of one rioter who "came rushing from the house, laden with plunder, was caught by Sergeant Burdick and knocked down; he had not released his hold of the thief ere a score of bullets whistled around his head, two of them lodging in the body of his prisoner, and six of the police fell at the discharge."

When the melèe was over, the Broadway Square policemen returned to headquarters. But the mob was not done with the Gibbons house yet. They regrouped and returned, finishing their plunder and setting fire to the house.

Abby and her daughter Sarah rushed back to New York. The family house was a smoldering ruin, and the process of filing claims with the city began. On July 24 the *New York Times* listed losses, including "from the dwelling of Mr. Gibbons, No. 19 Lamartine-place, a quantity of valuable household furniture, consisting in part of a marble-top table, a very superior clock, a mahogany dressing-case, a quantity of clothing, bedding &c., valued at over $800."

The list in the *Times* would amount to about $12,000 today; but it was only a fraction of the loss, which included the house itself. James claimed $1,600 in gas fixtures, alone. Abby wrote of the cruel losses: All of her father's papers were destroyed; over 2,000 books were gone as was her father's bookcase that had been in the family for over a century, his "pet piece of furniture."

Although Abby wanted to move away from the blackened scar in the row of homes on Lamartine Place, James was defiantly set on rebuilding. In addition to the $8,500 the family received in settlement from the city, $2,750 was donated by friends.

The blackened gash in the row of houses was filled with a new residence. The memories of the terror of July 1863 were too much to bear, however, and one-by-one the Gibbons' neighbors and relatives left Lamartine Place.

In 1865 the house was put up for sale. Three years later, in 1868, Mary Compton, a teacher in the Boys' Department of School No. 49 on East 37th Street was living here. In 1869 Professor Adolph Werner of the College of the City of New York took up residence. The German-born scholar would live here for four decades.

Werner had graduated from the College in 1857. By now he was Professor of German—a position he would hold for over half a century. Sometime prior to World War I he left the house—now numbered No. 339 West 29th Street—to live far uptown at No. 401 West End Avenue.

Throughout the twentieth century the Gibbons house was used by a variety of tenants for various activities. In 1932 the Domster Realty Corporation had its offices here, and in 1964 tenant Victor Santiago sold heroin from his apartment. The pretty park laid out by Mason and Torrey over a century earlier became part of the cooperative housing project for members of the International Ladies Garment Workers Union.

In 1968 the house was converted to two apartments per floor; little had changed outwardly from the 1864 building erected by the Gibbons. But that would not last.

In 2010 owners Tony and Nick Mamounas began an unauthorized fifth-floor penthouse addition. The Department of Buildings issued a stop-work order and told the brothers to remove the partially constructed addition.

The rebuilt No. 339 (third from right) complemented the earlier row of Greek Revival homes. By the turn of the century all of them had risen to four stories.

The men appealed and, while legal battles proceeded, Nick died, delaying the process. Community advocates and historians were incensed. One tenant called it "a tragedy" and told the *Daily News*, "It's a moral and historical landmark. It should be a source of pride for the city and not just be allowed to be desecrated in this way."

Historians were especially concerned about raising the roofline and interrupting the even flow of the buildings because it was across these roofs that the Gibbons sisters escaped in 1863. Tony Mamounas and his lawyer maintain that appeals are forthcoming; but in the meantime orders to remove the addition go ignored and the historic building is neglected and in disrepair. On January 29, 2012, the *Daily News* called it, "a dilapidated eyesore."

As the only certainly documented stop on the Underground Railroad in New York City the property with its unequaled and poignant history deserves better treatment.

MURRAY HILL

THE 1902 BOWDOIN STABLES
-149 E 38TH STREET

PHELPS-MORGAN MANSION
231 MADISON AVENUE

JOSEPH DE LAMAR MANSION,
233 MADISON AVENUE
AT 37TH STREET

The massive French house testified to its owner's wealth and position.

JOSEPH DE LAMAR MANSION

233 MADISON AVENUE AT 37TH STREET

By the turn of the last century, Manhattan's wealthiest citizens had abandoned most of the once-elegant residential neighborhoods below 50th Street. A few stalwart old-guard families remained along Washington Square; and despite increased commercial invasion, the Murray Hill neighborhood retained its reputation. That district was about to get a booster shot of prestige.

On April 17, 1901, a casual mention of a real estate sale appeared in the *New York Times*. "The Noyes estate has sold to J. R. De Lamar the four-story brownstone-front dwelling at 233 Madison Avenue, northeast corner of Thirty-seventh Street, 25 by 100."

Joseph Raphael De Lamar was a relative newcomer to Manhattan society. A Dutch-born merchant mariner, he was lured to the Far West in the 1870s by the prospects of mining. Unlike most of the hopeful miners, he struck it rich.

De Lamar moved to New York in the early 1890s laden with money and high hopes of entering society. He married Nellie Sands and the pair produced a daughter, Alice, in 1895. De Lamar bought the necessities—a yacht and cottage in Newport—and joined the exclusive clubs. Now he wanted a palace that reflected his financial station.

Three days after the *Times* reported on the Madison Avenue sale, mansion architect C. P. H. Gilbert filed plans "for the new fireproof residence" for De Lamar. Four months later the millionaire purchased the property next door, No. 235 Madison, which now gave him a plot with 100 feet along 37th Street and 49 feet along Madison Avenue. Directly across the street was the staid brownstone mansion of J. P. Morgan and it was soon to be overwhelmed.

Wealthy Murray Hill residents at the turn of the century were busily razing or radically remodeling their old homes from the Civil War period, transforming their property into stylish, up-to-date residences. De Lamar would go much further.

The nickel magnate had already embraced the new automobile over carriages and on August 22, 1902, as the house was rising, the *Times* reported on an innovation. "A unique feature of the new residence to be erected by J. R. De Lamar... is to be an automobile

The ballroom, like a slice of Versailles, featured a painted ceiling and gilded woodwork.

storage room in the vaults under the sidewalk, with an electric elevator for raising the vehicles to the street level." The millionaire's chauffeur would need only to drive up onto the sidewalk and the limousine would be lowered to a garage below street level.

Long before the mansion was completed in 1905, the De Lamars had divorced. Joseph moved into the new house with his daughter, Alice, now ten years old, and their nine servants. Gilbert had produced a gargantuan French palace six stories tall with a commanding mansard roof that overshadowed the fashionable old homes around it.

Joseph De Lamar haunted the circuit of art auctions, hauling back rare vases, tapestries, and paintings to the mansion. Young Alice was regularly mentioned in the society pages as she passed the age of her debut into society. But reportedly she was never really happy in the cavernous castle that was her father's most overt attempt at social inclusion. In 1917 the city assessed the De Lamar house at $400,000—about $4.5 million in today's dollars.

Thirteen years after moving into his new mansion, Joseph De Lamar died on December 1, 1918, of gallstones. Alice had already left Madison Avenue to serve in World War I as a volunteer mechanic and driver for the Red Cross Motor Corps.

The stalwart Alice would be a staunch advocate for affordable housing for working women. Having inherited an estate of about $10 million (her father also left at least that much to medical charities), Alice moved uptown to a 20-room, 7-bath flat at 270 Park Avenue. In 1919 the artwork, rare carpets, tapestries, and furnishings of the mansion were sold off in an auction ironically similar to the ones Joseph De Lamar attended.

The grand mansion would never again be a private residence. It became the clubhouse of the National Democratic Club until the Polish Government purchased it in 1973 for $900,000 as its New York Consulate.

The consulate initiated extensive restoration of both the exterior and interior of the house, and it still demands attention on the corner of Madison Avenue and 37th Street.

PHELPS-MORGAN MANSION

231 MADISON AVENUE

In the decade before the Civil War, wealthy New Yorkers in the fashionable Bond Street and St. John's Park neighborhoods were just beginning to consider leaving their refined homes as commercial enterprises slowly encroached.

Three connected families, however, evacuated early. The Phelps and Dodge families had made their immense fortunes mining copper. In 1847, John Jay Phelps, Isaac N. Phelps, and George D. Phelps purchased land from Mary Murray in what was known as Murray Hill. In 1850 George sold his lot to his nephew, William E. Dodge.

The men began construction on three dignified houses on Madison Road (later to become Madison Avenue) between 36th and 37th Streets. Completed around 1853, the impressive brownstone Anglo-Italian mansions shared gardens and stables. The Dodge and Phelps families were urban pioneers of a sort—Madison extended only five blocks further north, as far as 42nd Street.

Isaac Newton Phelps owned No. 231, the northernmost of the houses. Unlike his copper-mining family and neighbors, his wealth—estimated at the time at around $5 million, or nearly $130 million by today's standards—was made in hardware, banking, and real estate.

Phelps was already retired when he moved in with his wife, Anna, and their children. When he died thirty-five years later in 1888, the house and furnishings, valued at $175,000, were left to his daughter, Helen Louise Stokes. At the time of Phelps's death, J. Pierpont Morgan was living in the home built by John Jay Phelps, at the 36th Street corner. Morgan had purchased that residence in 1882.

Mabel Youngson was hired as a maid by Helen Stokes in 1892. Conspiring with her boyfriend, Arthur Morley, who was a servant a block away at No. 214, she slowly spirited costly items out of the mansion. After several months, Mrs. Stokes realized that over $2,000 worth of china, jewelry, and even rugs was missing. Youngson, however, gave the police the slip. Although much of the stolen property was recovered, the sticky-fingered maid escaped to England.

But by now the Lutheran Church had run out of money. A church spokesman said that because "money is no longer available today for building," it would keep the Morgan house "as is." The perilous situation, however, unnerved preservationists.

Beverly Moss Spatt, chairman of the Landmarks Preservation Commission was "shocked and disappointed" by the decision. Eminent preservation architect Giorgio Cavaglieri said the ruling "concerns itself with the fact that the owners of this building deserve the consideration of certain amounts of money. If they are entitled to compensation the local government has the responsibility to provide such compensation so that New York's citizens in the future, as well as the present, can at least have some living record of their visual heritage."

The Commission refused to surrender and in 1974 it re-designated the house a landmark.

The brownstone mansion serves as part of the Morgan Library today.

Refusing to be drab, the utilitarian structure combined architectural whimsy and elegance.

THE BOWDOIN STABLES

149 EAST 38TH STREET

In 1902, John W. Smyth sold the four-story house at 149 East 38th Street to real estate developer and clothing executive William R. H. Martin. In announcing the sale, the *New York Times* mentioned that, "The buyer will erect a private stable on the lot."

And indeed he did.

In New York City at the turn of the century, it was not merely one's good name that reflected one's position. The social elite strove to outdo one another in the finest homes, the best entertainments, and even in the appearance of their carriage houses. Utilitarian structures like private stables made their own statements regarding the social status of their owners—resulting in mini-chateaux and Renaissance palaces for horses.

Ralph Samuel Townsend received the commission for the proposed stable. The architect, who was best known for his apartment buildings and hotels, gave a whimsical nod to New York's roots by designing a Flemish Revival brick structure with a stepped gable, each step supporting a swirling stone console bracket. Stone detailing stood out starkly from the brick façade. Townsend added two full-relief wreathed horse's heads above the first floor cornice and a large sculpted bulldog's head high above the street.

An ornate carved stone frame surrounded an oval window directly below the dog's head, and behind the gable rose a tiled mansard roof.

Financier George S. Bowdoin, who lived nearby on Park Avenue near 36th Street, purchased the building in 1907 at a time when little-by-little motorcars replaced horse-drawn vehicles. Bowdoin's horses lived on the first floor while his coachmen lived upstairs. The banker's elegant carriages lined up along one side of the stables.

Edith Bowdoin inherited the property when her father died in 1913. By now, however, it would seem that it was no longer being used as a carriage house. The 1909 *Directory of the Breeders and Exhibitors of Dogs in the United States and Canada* listed W. Cox as running his fox terrier breeding business from here.

A carved bulldog stares down over a beautifully carved window surround.

OPPOSITE PAGE On either side carved horse heads poke through stone wreaths.

In 1918, Edith Bowdoin had the horse paddocks removed and converted the lower portion of the building into a garage. After her death the property was sold to George Nichols, who stored his four private vehicles in the garage portion while renting out the residence above.

The unique, ornate building lived a humdrum existence through most of the 20th century until it was gutted around 1984. The new owner, who paid $2 million for the structure, installed multiple skylights and created soaring spaces—some 20 feet high. But after the renovation and just before he could move in, he married and moved to California. The 6,000-square-foot residence with its sleek spiral staircase and open spaces was rented to Jane Nichols Page.

Then in 1997, Donald and Ruth Saff purchased the property for about $3.4 million. Where horses once munched hay, the Saffs now hung artwork by Lichtenstein, Rauschenberg, and Nancy Graves.

The Saffs used No. 149 as their personal gallery/home/office until 2002 when it became the Gabarron Foundation's Carriage House Center for the Arts. The non-profit association was founded that same year to promote "the cultural wealth

and identity of both Spain and America," and hosted exhibitions and lectures from the space.

When the Carriage House Center for the Arts moved out in May 2011, the astounding survivor was on the market again, this time for $14 million. Townsend's flamboyant Dutch Renaissance carriage house, landmarked in 1997, is today a unique single-family home.

TIMES SQUARE

FATHER DUFFY STATUE
TIMES SQUARE

FATHER DUFFY

ALGONQUIN HOTEL
59 WEST 44TH STREET

PARAMOUNT BUILDING
BROADWAY AND 43RD STREET,
TIMES SQUARE

A skyscraper in its day, the Algonquin's faceted bays helped catch passing breezes.

ALGONQUIN HOTEL

59 WEST 44TH STREET

The 44th Street block between Fifth and Sixth Avenues had, by the turn of the century, drastically changed. The street that had been lined with two-story stables and carriage houses now boasted the exclusive Harvard Club and the New York Yacht Club, as well as high-toned residence hotels.

Albert Foster planned another residence hotel at 59 West 44th Street to be called the Puritan. He commissioned architect Goldwin Starrett to create an up-to-date design intended to attract well-heeled tenants. Starrett embellished his neo-Renaissance-inspired façade with trendy Beaux Arts touches. Above the two-story limestone base, red brick and limestone were interrupted by soaring, continuous cast-metal bays nine stories tall. The bay windows not only added depth and interest to the otherwise flat façade, they increased air flow to rooms that could be stifling in hot, humid months.

As the hotel was still rising, Foster began hiring his staff, among whom was 31-year-old Frank Case. Having already worked for nearly a decade in the well-known Taylor's Hotel in Jersey City, Case knew his way around the hotel industry. One of his first concerns was the name of the hotel.

The clerk realized that the word "puritan" had repressive connotations that could possibly discourage potential tenants. A particularly American word, he felt, might be more advisable. After combing through manuscripts at the public library, he came up with the Native American term "Algonquin" and convinced his boss to change the name.

The hotel opened on November 22, 1902, with already three-fourths of the apartments occupied. The *New York Tribune* was highly impressed, calling it "the last step in excellence in this class of structure." The critic said, "The elegance of the structure, the perfection of its embodied details, combined with the letter-perfect house service of this new family hotel, bid fair to make it lead all of its class."

The *Tribune* felt that the new hotel was the solution to "this vexatious servant problem." Even if, said the paper, "you are a householder, with ever and ever so nice a home in the exclusive upper East and West Side districts of Manhattan" you would have troubles with live-in staff. "It is these folk who keep one's house in a wild confusion and bring wrinkles and worries to its managers," it said.

According to the *Tribune*, "This house gives you your home always heated at seasonable temperatures, always well lighted and spickly clean, and your servants, always quiet, thoroughly trained, respectful and efficient."

Residents could either order meals served in their apartments from a "menu card" or take meals in the large restaurant on the main floor. The board for private servants was an additional $7 a week. Each apartment had a telephone that connected it with the hotel offices as well as the city telephone service. Hotel staff was available to summon a carriage or order theater or train tickets. An in-house physician, barber, hairdresser, or manicurist would make calls to rooms; the house valet attended to everyone's shoes and made sure newspapers and magazines were delivered promptly.

The apartments were outfitted with waxed, oak floors, and mahogany woodwork that included mantels and built-in bookcases. Each bedroom had its own bathroom, "a wonderfully complete affair in white enamel with all the latest kinds of plumbing and toilet appliances," said the *Tribune*—a remarkable luxury of the day. Annual rates for the apartments ranged from $420 for a one-bedroom and bath to $2,520 for a luxurious suite of three bedrooms, private dining room, parlor, library, three bathrooms, and private hallway.

Although Albert Foster owned the hotel, it was Frank Case who embraced it as his own. Although the hotel was just a block from fashionable Fifth Avenue, it sat an equal distance from the Times Square theater district. Case, who as a teenager had worked as an usher in a Buffalo vaudeville theater, was intent on luring the theatrical crowd. Actor Douglas Fairbanks became a close friend of Case and was one of the first to haunt the Algonquin, along with stage idol of the time John Drew.

In 1904 the Sixth Avenue Railroad Depot that stretched from 43rd to 44th Street was demolished and in its place rose the gargantuan New York Hippodrome, a 5,600-seat theater directly across 44th Street from the Algonquin. Frank Case later remarked that the theater's opening was "an important event for us."

Soon the hotel was home to theatrical legends including Booth Tarkington, Sinclair Lewis, and John and Ethel Barrymore—laying the groundwork for theatrical and literary history.

By 1908 the guests of the hotel were mainly transient. An advertisement of that year noted, "The Algonquin desires to increase its family patronage. Less than twenty percent of the Algonquin is occupied by permanent guests." It stressed the advantage of the hotel to permanent residents: "It affords better service than the regular apartment hotel, while the orderly hum of industry, the coming and going of prominent people, makes hotel life interesting and disturbs not at all the home like atmosphere of refinement." The advertisement was signed "Frank M. Case, Jr."

The atmosphere of refinement was dashed on October 13, 1912, when screams emanated from the rooms of Charlotte Walker. The actress had awakened to find a man in her room, and when Frank Case flung open the door, he saw a shadowy figure on the fire escape. Hotel staff captured the burglar and he was arrested.

He was later found to be the 37-year-old Frenchman, Paul Renaud, who had appeared in the lobby earlier that day. When he was told the rate of a room, he admitted he could not afford the price and it was assumed he had left.

Magistrate McQuade, on hearing the testimony of all parties, was about to release the prisoner, saying there was no evidence that he intended burglary. A room key, in fact, had been found on Renaud—something Frank Case could not explain away. But at the last minute Case told the judge that "indecent postal cards had been found in the possession of the man." Sergeant McNierney of the East 52nd Street Station confirmed this and the prisoner was held on $500 bail.

Having racy French postcards was, it seems, a greater offense than breaking and entering.

In 1917, years ahead of Prohibition, Case closed the hotel bar because he feared the presence of a saloon in his establishment might spoil the atmosphere of refinement he cultivated.

Although he aggressively wooed writers and actors, Case found they were not always ideal guests. When one playwright accumulated a hotel bill of $2,200, Case tossed him out. In an attempt at payment the writer gave him a manuscript which turned out to be a stage play. Case made an agreement with another playwright living in the Algonquin to edit it on a 50/50 basis. The resulting play, *Fine Feather*, ran a full season on Broadway, netting Case $5,500 in royalties.

Case's daughter, Margaret, was born in room 1206 in 1904, and as she grew she became the darling of the famous guests. Years later she would remember the time that John Barrymore reacted to a rumor that she had a crush on a theater cad. The actor whisked the young girl away in a carriage and, while driving through Central Park demanded that she "dismiss the young man immediately."

The astonished Margaret explained that she had never met the actor in question and had only seen him once on stage. Barrymore, realizing that he had been duped by a braggart, responded, "Oh, that ham!"

In 1919 a short, chubby newspaperman with wire-rimmed glasses was given an innocuous assignment of writing a critique on the Algonquin Hotel for a Sunday edition. It was a job that would make the Algonquin a household word across the nation.

Alexander Woollcott did not gush on about the Algonquin. He called it "a little, unpretentious hotel, tucked away on a side street." While he mentioned some of the celebrities who lived here, it was the kitchen's apple pie that caught his attention.

Lured by the siren song of the pie, he suggested to his every-Saturday-lunch partners, Franklin Pierce Adams and Heywood Broun, that they meet at the hotel.

Before long the group grew to include Robert Benchley, Brock Pemberton, and Harold Ross. It was the beginning of the legendary Algonquin Round Table.

Frank Case recognized the importance of the group's patronage and assigned it a private corner of the Oak Room. As the group outgrew its private niche, Case moved them to a large, round table in the Rose Room. By the 1920s the Round Table included the acerbic Dorothy Parker, as well as S. J. Perelman, Ruth Gordon, Tallulah Bankhead, Irving Berlin, Russel Crouse, and a score of other luminaries.

The Round Table blistered with literary debates and poker games (the second most popular diversion). Upstairs, Case provided a room for the poker parties that often extended from Saturday nights through Sunday afternoons.

With the onset of the Great Depression the Round Table quietly disintegrated. Many of the writers and critics were forced to leave New York City for Los Angeles. The personal toll of the economic situation was vividly expressed in 1929 when a dapperly dressed man ordered a meal in the dining room. Wearing a morning coat and gray vest, with spats and a bowler hat, he ate in silence. When he had finished his coffee and pie, he removed a small pearl-handled handgun from his pocket and put a bullet into his head.

Frank Case purchased the hotel for $717,000 in 1932, making official what everyone already knew: he owned the Algonquin.

In 1943 the locally famous François was the hotel's sommelier. After years of serving and choosing the correct wines for discriminating patrons, his health failed and he necessarily stepped down from his position. Waitress Elizabeth Bird wanted the job, although her only training in wines came from reading a book.

Case gave her the job, insisting that she be called "Francine."

The concept of a woman performing the job of a sommelier was a bit shocking. The *New York Times* called Francine "probably the only woman in New York with the privilege of telling fastidious men which wines to drink." The newspaper could not resist the opportunity to drop a sexist remark, however. "A native New Yorker, she speaks in restrained tones and has learned the knack—the envy of many a wife—of being respectful yet not obsequious; of getting her way without offending male vanity."

Frank Case died in 1946 at the age of 76. In addition to an Algonquin Hotel cookbook, he had written two books, the 1938 *Tales of a Wayward Inn*, that documented anecdotes of famous and not-famous guests; and *Do Not Disturb*, written two years later as a sequel.

Ben B. and Mary Bodne purchased the hotel and would run it for years. Sir Laurence Olivier reportedly adored Mary's chicken soup. The Bodnes carefully preserved the traditions of the Algonquin. Harry Connick, Jr., made his New York debut here and, even as the hotel became a bit dowdy, it retained its fabled atmosphere.

New York magazine, on February 7, 1977, wrote, "If Mo Udall, Tom Stoppard, Kyle Rote and Ellen Burstyn are all in the same room, the room must be in New

WEST FORTY-FOURTH ST.,
NEW YORK
FOYER
ALGONQUIN HOTEL
FRANK M. CASE, JR.

An early postcard depicts the comfortable foyer.

York. If your college roommate's first husband and the person you're thinking might be right to back your next project and a woman you mistake for your Great-aunt Martha are also in the room, then the room is the lobby of the Algonquin Hotel."

As the twenty-first century dawned, performing in the Oak Room was a great distinction for cabaret and nightclub singers. In February of 2012 it was still one of Manhattan's three major cabaret supper clubs.

That month the Oak Room closed as part of the renovation of the entire hotel. New Yorkers familiar with the 32-year-old supper club were dismayed at the announcement that upon the hotel's scheduled reopening in May 2012 the Oak Room would be a "lounge." Yet, few structures in Manhattan—or perhaps the nation—have a theatrical and literary history as rich as that of the Algonquin Hotel.

ART DECO
PARAMOUNT BUILDING
TIMES SQUARE AT BROADWAY
AND 43RD STREET

By the end of World War I the motion picture industry had begun a serious migration from New York to California. Yet in 1926 when Paramount Pictures decided to build its new headquarters, President Adolf Zukor chose Times Square for the site. The motion picture giant would make its mark on Broadway—the capital of the American theater.

Architects C. W. and George L. Rapp, of the Chicago-based firm Rapp and Rapp, had designed several Midwestern movie theaters. Now they were given the substantial Paramount commission.

In May 1926 the cornerstone was laid by Mayor Jimmy Walker. Sealed inside were three copper boxes containing the front pages of New York's morning newspapers, three $5 gold coins, two Paramount feature films, and newsreels of Admiral Byrd's polar expedition. Thomas Edison sent a letter of congratulations.

Here on Broadway between 43rd and 44th Streets, Rapp and Rapp produced a 33-story Art Deco tower, stair-stepping upward to an enormous four-faced clock surmounted by an illuminated globe. Stars replaced numerals on the clock faces, echoing the stars in the Paramount logo.

Paramount spent $13.5 million on their new headquarters, the tallest building on Broadway north of the Woolworth Building. At night the globe could be seen from as far away as New Jersey.

On the Broadway side an ornate, curved marquee hung over the entrance to the theater. The lobby inside was modeled after the Paris Opera. Two grand, sweeping staircases curved upwards on either side. An enormous crystal chandelier hung from a baroque ceiling supported by marble columns.

The 3,664-seat auditorium was neo-Renaissance in style, with classical busts and statues in recessed niches, gilded detailing, and a frescoed ceiling. Red carpeting led to the stage hung with stories-high red velvet draperies. The orchestra pit was situated on hydraulic elevators, enabling it to be raised and lowered as needed.

The mountain-like design was meant to reflect the Paramount logo.

The ornate marquee, restored in 2000 after being scrapped, is seen in an early postcard.

The coup-de-grâce was the "Dowager Empress," one of the largest pipe organs ever built by Wurlitzer. Music accompanying the silent films emanated from the organ's thirty-three tons of pipes and thirty-six ranks.

Opening on November 19, 1926, the theater took in a staggering $800,000 the first week.

Paramount used its New York theater to première many of its films, introducing stars such as Mae West, Claudette Colbert, and William Powell. But the Great Depression made moviegoing an avoidable luxury. Through the early 1930s the venue was barely profitable. In an effort to boost attendance, the Paramount's managers added live music as the Swing Era took hold. In December 1935, Glen Gray's orchestra played here. And the public loved it.

Big bands became a staple of the Paramount, offering the music of the biggest names in American swing: Tommy Dorsey, Xavier Cugat, Fred Waring, Benny

Goodman, Glenn Miller, the Andrews Sisters, Guy Lombardo, Eddy Duchin, Harry James, Phil Spitalny, and Gene Krupa among them. As the years passed, entertainers incuding Jack Benny, Dean Martin and Jerry Lewis, and Frank Sinatra would work the Paramount audience.

In 1944, with the blackout orders that accompanied America's entry into World War II, both the clock and the globe were painted black. They would remain that way until their restoration in 1996.

Famous 1950s music promoter Alan Freed used the Paramount to stage live rock 'n' roll shows, spotlighting such hot new talent as Buddy Holly and the Crickets. Here, too, Elvis Presley's first movie, *Love Me Tender*, premiered on November 15, 1956. Thousands of fans crushed onto Broadway on opening night, under a 40-foot Elvis Presley cutout.

The popularity of television in the 1960s and the decline of the Broadway neighborhood devastated the theater's revenues. After the final screening of *The Carpetbaggers* on August 4, 1964, Paramount padlocked the doors to the palatial theater.

Within weeks the grand staircase was gone. The frescoes were destroyed. The chandeliers were sold. All traces of the lavish movie palace were obliterated as the space was converted into stores and offices. The mammoth organ was moved to a Wichita, Kansas, convention center. The familiar marquee that had once held the over-sized cut-out of Elvis Presley and announced the movies of Gary Cooper, Gloria Swanson, and Rudolph Valentino was removed and destroyed.

Then in 2000, the World Wrestling Federation leased 47,500 square feet of the Paramount Building, spending $38 million to create WWF New York—a wrestling-themed restaurant, retail store, and club. Astoundingly, the group painstakingly recreated the original Paramount Theater marquee and arch at a cost of $8 million, including the Paramount logo. Although WWF New York was relatively short-lived, the Paramount arch and marquee survive.

The 33-story Paramount Building is an iconic presence in the Broadway Theater District. Every day at 1:45 p.m. and 7:45 p.m. the giant clock atop the building chimes, alerting Broadway theatergoers that they have fifteen minutes before curtain.

FATHER FRANCIS P. DUFFY STATUE

TIMES SQUARE

FATHER DUFFY

"I am a very Irish, very Catholic, very American person, if anybody challenges my convictions. But normally and let alone, I am just plain human."

And that is how Father Francis Patrick Duffy described himself in the preface to his 1919 biography, *Father Duffy's Story*. New Yorkers, however, disagreed. Father Duffy was anything but "just plain human."

Things started out calmly enough for the priest. He was ordained in 1896 and, upon graduating from the Catholic University of America in Washington, D.C., he was sent to St. Joseph's Seminary in New York as Professor of Psychology and Ethics. Duffy had been an Army chaplain during the Spanish-American War and, after becoming pastor of Our Savior Catholic Church in the Bronx, he was made chaplain of the 165th National Guard Unit of the 42nd Division—formerly the 69th Infantry Regiment. His appointment came the same year that World War I broke out in Europe.

And that's when things changed for the Irish priest.

The unit had been dubbed "The Fighting 69th" by Confederate General Robert E. Lee and was remembered in an Irish-American folk tune, "The Fighting 69th," for its Civil War exploits. The 165th would always be the 69th to its soldiers.

With America's entry into the war in 1917, the regiment was shipped off to fight overseas. Among the soldiers was poet Joyce Kilmer, a sergeant. Aboard ship transporting the troops across the Atlantic, he described the men lining up for confession with Father Duffy "as long as the mess-line."

If officers expected the chaplain to wait passively for the soldiers to return so he could administer rites and dispense priestly wisdom, they were wrong. By the end of the war, Duffy was the most highly decorated chaplain in U.S. Army history—earning the Distinguished Service Cross and the Distinguished Service Medal from the U.S., and the *Legion d'Honneur* and the *Croix de Guerre* from the French government.

While on the front lines, Joyce Kilmer was writing the story of the regiment in battle. A year after the unit's deployment, he was killed at the Second Battle of the Marne in 1918, at 31 years of age. Father Duffy picked up Kilmer's notes and finished the project. The result was Father Duffy's Story: *A Tale of Humor and Heroism, of*

Life and Death with the Fighting Sixty-Ninth. Published in 1919, it credited both Duffy and Kilmer as authors.

When the war was finally over, Duffy quietly returned to New York City to take up his duties as pastor of Holy Cross Church in Hell's Kitchen, just a block from Times Square—a gritty area of mostly impoverished Irish immigrants. He died on June 26, 1932.

Almost immediately a movement was begun to honor the hero priest with a monument. On September 10, 1935, the Municipal Art Commission gave preliminary approval to a model of a statue designed by sculptor Charles Keck to be erected in the large, triangular traffic island in Times Square where Broadway and Seventh Avenue intersect above 47th Street.

The dramatic and powerful design depicted Duffy in the uniform of the 69th, helmet at his feet, holding a Bible. Behind the soldier-priest a monolithic green granite Celtic cross rose.

The monument was completed in the spring of 1937 and as the city prepared for its unveiling, renowned photographer Berenice Abbott chanced upon the tightly wrapped statue one day in April. The unusual subject was too much to pass up and Abbot began assembling her tripod and setting up the shot.

Charles Keck chose to depict the priest in a decidedly non-clerical posture.

Before long a curious crowd assembled to watch the photographer's work. A Times Square beat cop was less interested in her art than in the growing throng. Berating her for causing a public disturbance, he ordered her to move on. Abbott took one hasty shot and packed up.

"I wasn't smart about fighting back then," she later lamented.

A few days later, on May 2, the statue was unveiled. "Before the eyes of 30,000 persons massed in Times Square yesterday," reported the *New York Times*, "[as] white

The statue stands amid a bustling mid-century Times Square.

surpliced altar boys held aloft a crucifix and candles, there was unveiled the statue of a Roman Catholic priest in the uniform of a soldier of the A.E.F."

The finished bronze statue is nearly 8 feet tall and the green granite cross tops 17 feet. The traffic island on which it sits was renamed Father Duffy Square. Only eight years after it was dedicated, the statue was nearly lost when the city considered melting it down in 1943 for scrap metal for the war effort.

Father Duffy Square has seen dramatic changes since that spring day in 1937 when the monument was unveiled. Throngs of tourists and New Yorkers alike pass the monument daily in bustling Times Square where the modern TKTS booth now forms the statue's backdrop.

MIDTOWN

1240 SIXTH AVENUE

13 AND 15 WEST 54TH STREET

MEDICAL ARTS
BUILDING
57 WEST 57TH STREET

ROCKEFELLER CENTER'S DAVID VS GOLIATH

1240 SIXTH AVENUE

Unlike its haughty neighbor Fifth Avenue to the east, Sixth Avenue in the late nineteenth century was decidedly blue collar. The Sixth Avenue elevated tracks blocked sunlight, and the passing trains spewed cinders and smoke. Between 43rd and 44th Streets sat the Sixth Avenue car stables, and at the northeast corner of 49th Street was a saloon owned by three Irishmen.

Patrick "Paddy" Daly, Daniel Hurley, and his brother Connie Hurley took a long-term lease on the four-story, red-brick building in 1892. They established a partnership and opened a saloon called Hurley Brothers and Daly. The block was lined with similar Victorian structures, terminating on the opposite end of the block with a three-story brick building owned by the Boronowsky family.

Things went well for the partners who reportedly shared the heavy-drinking habits of their clientele at the 54-foot-long mahogany bar with bronze fittings. But 27 years later, as with every other saloon in the city, the foundations of Hurley Brothers and Daly would be rocked by Prohibition. Prompted by well-intentioned reformers who believed that the elimination of alcohol would result in reduced crime, increased morality, improved public health, and financial stability, Prohibition had other effects. Thousands of New Yorkers were suddenly unemployed—bartenders, tavern owners, brewery workers, and waitresses. Scores of hotels and restaurants, unable to survive were forced to close.

But the headstrong Irishmen who ran what was known as Hurley's would not let a simple Federal law get in their way. Within five years after the enactment of the Volstead Act there were an estimated 100,000 speakeasies in New York City. Hurley's was one of them.

The saloon was moved to the back of the building with an unmarked entrance on 49th Street. The front section was rented to Greek florists. For additional income and camouflage the upstairs was leased to Mrs. Shea, who rented out "furnished rooms"; a barber shop, a fruit stand, and a luggage store shared ground-floor space with the hidden saloon.

But there was an even bigger problem looming for the Hurley brothers. John D. Rockefeller, Jr., had begun aggressively buying up a staggering twenty-two

The Victorian
structure is
dwarfed by
the soaring
Rockefeller
Center buildings
around it.

acres of midtown property, right in the middle of Fifth Avenue's most exclusive
district, for a seemingly implausible project: Rockefeller Center. One by one he
purchased buildings from Fifth to Sixth Avenue between 48th and 51st Streets. In
the stranglehold of the Great Depression, few could resist the offer to convert real
estate to cash.

None, in fact, except John F. Maxwell, grandson of John F. Boronowsky, who
owned the three-story building at the opposite end of the block from Hurley's and,
of course, the feisty Irishmen themselves. In June 1931, Maxwell sent word to
Rockefeller that he would not sell "at any price."

Daniel Hurley and Patrick Daly did not own their building, but still had a long-
term lease. They worded their refusal to budge as a veiled offer. Rockefeller's agents
had managed to buy the building so the saloon-keepers, realizing that the repeal of
Prohibition was only months away, requested a lease buyout: $250 million.

According to Liz Trotta in her book *Fighting for Air: In the Trenches with Television News*,
Connie Hurley would later proclaim in his Irish brogue, "I've seen sonofabitchin'
Rockefellers come and sonofabitchin' Rockefellers go and no sonofabitchin'
Rockefeller's gonna tear down my bar."

And, indeed, no Rockefeller tore down Hurley's bar.

Construction had already begun on the gargantuan Art Deco complex of nineteen
buildings on. The block of 49th to 50th Streets, Sixth Avenue to Fifth Avenue was
eventually demolished, leaving only the two brick Victorian buildings standing on
opposite corners of a devastated landscape.

The RCA Building—70 stories tall—rose around Hurley's, diminishing the bar
building only in height. A reader wrote to *New York* magazine decades later calling

Hurley's "a four-story David thumbing its nose at the Goliath that was Rockefeller Center," and Jack Kerouac deemed it "a real old building that nobody ever notices because it forms the pebble at the hem of the shoe of the immense tall man which is the RCA Building."

And then a strange thing happened to the Irish saloon that had been the watering hole for blue-collar workers and immigrants. It became the watering hole for radio, television, newspaper, and sports celebrities as well as tourists and midtown workers. As the century progressed, the old-fashioned saloon and its crusty Irish owner ("Old Man Hurley" lived to an extremely ripe old age), as well as the convenient location in Rockefeller Center, made Hurley's a favorite. Liz Trotta noted, "You never knew who would be standing next to your lifting elbow at Hurley's. Jason Robards, Jonathan Winters, jazz musicians from the local clubs and the 'Tonight' show, starlets, football players, the lot."

Johnny Carson made the Hurley name nationally familiar while he did his show live from Rockefeller Center. It was the bar in all of his Ed McMahon drinking jokes. David Letterman did several on-air visits to the bar. NBC technicians haunted the place so regularly that among themselves it was known as Studio 1-H.

Hurley's was known as a place where status was left at the door. Mayor John Lindsay stopped in once, only to be hissed by the patrons. When Henry Kissinger and two bodyguards got noisy, they were ejected by the bartender "for rowdy behavior."

But nothing in New York City is permanent and in 1975 the business of Hurley Brothers and Daly was sold. Journalist William Safire spoke for New Yorkers in an article mourning the loss. The mahogany bar was removed to a Third Avenue restaurant and, as Nancy Arum wrote in her letter to *New York* magazine that year, "a pretend old-fashioned bar now stands where the real old-fashioned bar once was."

The pretend old-fashioned bar took the name Hurley's and, most likely, tourists never noticed the change. But proximity, tradition, or habit still brought the Rockefeller Center workers and celebrities into the bar until September 2, 1999. That night owner Adrien Barbey served the last glass of beer in the bar that had stood at Sixth Avenue and 49th Street for 102 years.

The 64-year-old bar owner, having undergone stomach and heart surgery, decided to retire. On the final day of operation, the windowsills were crammed with floral arrangements sent by patrons. As the last hours ticked away, loyal customers took away menus and matchbooks as mementos.

Today, the red-brick building is painted gray—a no-doubt purposeful near-match to the limestone façade of the RCA (now GE Building) that wraps around it. Where three Irishmen once served beer—legally and illegally—to tough, boisterous working men, a pristine bakery sells cupcakes.

The little buildings flanking the RCA Building stand as monuments to independent businessmen who refused to be bullied by a millionaire with limitless power.

MEDICAL ARTS BUILDING
57 WEST 57TH STREET

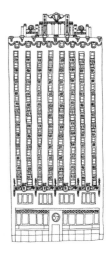

In 1928, West 57ᵗʰ Street was no longer the mishmash of small brick buildings and undeveloped lots it had been a generation earlier. Midtown was booming and 57th Street had earned a reputation as an arts center, with Carnegie Hall, the Architectural League, the Fine Arts Society, and the Rodin Studios building, among others, lining the thoroughfare.

The fine arts would meet the medical arts that year when Alain E. White's Medical Arts Building, also known as the Professional Centre Building, was completed at 57 West 57th Street. Designed by the architectural firm of Warren & Wetmore, the 18-story structure was specifically intended for physicians, dentists, and related medical professionals.

Immediately private doctors—some with their own mini-hospitals and sanitariums—and medical institutions moved in. The Medical Arts Sanitarium opened on the entire 14th floor on November 21, 1928, run by Dr. George E. Browning (the facility was sometimes referred to as "Dr. Browning's Sanitarium"). Marketing itself as "Luxury at Moderate Cost," no room cost more than $10 per day. "The institution is open to all physicians, where they may treat their own medical and surgical cases," reported the *New York Times*. The article added, "All rooms are equipped with radios."

Shortly after opening, the Medical Arts Sanitarium was the scene of tragedy. 27-year-old Esther Glasser was admitted after she fell into deep depression when her hopes of becoming a teacher were dashed after suffering a nervous breakdown (brought on, it was felt, over-study).

On February 3, 1929, she told her nurse that she felt ill. When the nurse left the room to go for medicine, she jumped from her bed and headed toward the open window. Her sister, Leah, grabbed her arm, but she broke free. A taxi driver, Martin Newman, saw Esther's body hit the pavement 14 floors below the window.

But more drama was unfolding above the Sanitarium level. Upon the completion of the structure Department of Buildings records documented, "two housekeeping apartments" on the 17th and 18th floors. The two luxurious penthouses in a building

High above street level Edna and Charles lived their dramatic and peculiar lives.

of medical offices and hospital rooms would be the scene of astonishing drama.

Albert Champion had been a professional bicycle racer but he acquired a staggering fortune when he invented the spark plug. On a business trip to New York the aging and married Champion ran into the much younger Edna Crawford—a girl who came to the big city looking for a wealthy man.

As described in lurid detail by Doris Lane in her *Ghoulies and Ghosts: The Haunted Penthouse*, before long Champion persuaded his wife to agree to a divorce; giving her $1 million to sweeten the deal. He married Edna, but the autumn-spring romance quickly soured. Intensely jealous, he lavished clothing and jewels on his new wife, but he refused to provide her with her own spending money.

While the pair was in Paris, Edna met the dashing Charles Brazelle and started an affair. Ironically, Brazelle was a fortune hunter just as Edna had been. Champion learned of the affair and threatened to leave Edna penniless. When he found the lovers together at the Crillon Bar on October 26, 1927, a violent confrontation ensued during which Brazelle punched the older man. A few hours later the 47-year old Champion was found dead in his hotel.

Edna and Charles Brazelle persuaded authorities that Champion had died of a "weak heart" and the investigation went no further.

Edna, now $12 million richer, returned to New York with the still-married Brazelle in tow. He expressed his wish to live in a glitzy modern apartment and fell in love with the penthouse of the Medical Arts Building. But the apartments were not for rent—so Edna purchased the entire building for $1.3 million in cash.

Decorators and architects were hired to renovate the two apartments, including a secret stairway to connect them. Edna took the upper apartment, Charles the lower. Reportedly, the terraces were landscaped with exotic plants, and the interiors were overdone, with gold and silver walls, and fountains under "artificial moonlight." Edna's carved bed featured a canopy of gold cloth made from $30,000 worth of Russian clerical vestments.

In one room Edna commissioned a 40-foot mural depicting a Venetian carnival. The central figures were she and Charles, with Edna stark naked but for a pair of high heels and a mask. Elsewhere antique European tapestries, custom floors, marble mantels, and stained-glass windows were installed.

The remodeling of the apartments would take years. In the meantime "Charlie" Brazelle installed a brokerage office on the second floor to handle his accounts and collect the building rents; and in 1934 he opened a nightclub in the basement. Based on a club in Paris it even took the same name, the Boeuf sur le Toit. The opening was held on December 13 that year with a benefit dinner and show for the Social Service Department of the Roosevelt Hospital and the Post Contagion Unit of the Speedwell Society. The *New York Times* headline read "New Club's Opening to Attract Society, Many Dinners Will be Given at Tomorrow's Celebration in the Boeuf Sur Le Toit."

Things weren't going so happily upstairs, however. Like Edna's marriage to Albert Champion, this relationship had taken a dark turn. Charlie kept Edna a prisoner in her apartment and hired French servants who reported her movements to him. The pair had repeated drunken fights, and during one such incident he threw a telephone and struck her. When Edna's relatives discovered what was going on, they had him ejected from the building and hired bodyguards to protect her. Charlie moved into the New York Athletic Club.

But Charlie had keys to all the medical offices and would sometimes hide for days in the building, moving from one suite to another. Finally, on the same night she died from drugs and alcohol (and a telephone injury), Charlie made his final attempt to get to her. Supposedly, the bodyguards caught him and he was flung from her bedroom window onto the terrace below.

On December 19, 1935 Charles Brazelle died in Flower Fifth Hospital of heart disease.

The bizarre apartments high above 57th Street sat unoccupied for some time. Carlton Alsop was a radio and film producer who was close friends with celebrities such as Judy Garland. Just married, he rented the Champion apartment for himself and his bride, a relative of Mrs. John D. Rockefeller, Jr. He was drawn, too, to the terraces which would provide outdoor space for his four Great Danes.

The two top floors were redecorated into a stylish, sleek home. The gaudy, overblown décor was ripped out—all except for, oddly enough, the 40-foot mural with the nude Edna Champion. But the atmosphere was strained.

The dogs whined and stared at windows or walls during the night and Mrs. Alsop exhibited strange behavior. Both of the newlyweds reported hearing high-heeled footsteps in the night and the sounds of arguing. Within a year an unnerved Mrs. Alsop packed her bags and moved out.

After his brief marriage failed Alsop threw cocktail parties to cheer himself up. According to Danton Walker in his *Spooks Deluxe*, "At one of these a guest went upstairs to visit the bathroom and returned, white and shaking, unable to explain what had come over him. On another occasion, a woman guest—an English-woman with a high-sounding title—vowed that someone had followed her down the stairs. When all present denied any complicity, she indignantly stated that she 'disliked practical jokes.'"

The sound of footsteps eventually drove Alsop nearly mad and he ended up in the hospital below his penthouse. After his treatment and release, he sublet the penthouse "at no matter what financial loss."

While the bizarre stories played out in the penthouse apartments, the medical offices continued on downstairs. In April 1930 the 57 West Fifty-seventh Street Sanitarium opened on four floors "devoted to inexpensive rooms" for middle-class patients, as reported in the *New York Times*.

"No city in the world provides better than New York for the rich and the poor classes, but the middle class has been absolutely neglected," said Dr. Max S. Rhode, a director.

In 1938 the nightclub below ground became La Conga, deemed by the Times "a new Cuban club." *The New Yorker* said, "If your soulful moods involve clasping your loved one in your arms and swaying to rumba music, La Conga at 57 West Fifty-seventh Street has the atmosphere."

Later the club would become Dario's La Martinique and it was here that Danny Kaye made his New York debut (for $250 a week for a one-week booking).

Today there are still some medical offices in the building, but the private sanitariums and hospitals are long gone. The former penthouse apartments became home to an art gallery, fordProject, in 2011. While art and sculpture now fills the rooms where lovers fought and died, for those addicted to ghost stories the address still holds special meaning.

Gilded decoration embellishes the lower floors of the building some think is haunted.

HARDENBERGH'S TWINS

13 AND 15 WEST 54TH STREET

As Midtown Manhattan developed, comfortable upper-class homes rose on the side streets that branched off Fifth Avenue. When St. Luke's Hospital (which had extended far down 54th and 55th Streets from Fifth Avenue) was demolished in 1896, wealthy businessman William Murray purchased the plots at Nos. 13 and 15 West 54th.

Murray commissioned the noted architect Henry J. Hardenbergh to design two tasteful residences on the site. The architect, who had designed numerous well-known structures in the city including the Waldorf and the Astoria Hotels and the Dakota apartment building, designed near-matching homes in a Renaissance-inspired style.

Clad in limestone with oriel windows, heavy carvings, and sweeping, paired staircases, the homes were both grand and picturesque. While the two houses, completed in 1897, were nearly mirror images, No. 13 was slightly taller.

The wealthy and socially prominent widow of stockbroker Walter S. Neilson, Jessie, purchased No. 13, living here until 1901 when she rented it fully-furnished to John D. Rockefeller, Jr., on September 25. Rockefeller was to be married to Abbie Green Aldrich within two weeks and the house was appropriate for the new couple both in location and prestige. The groom-to-be signed a three-year lease on the house, which was conveniently across the street from his father's home at 4 West 54th Street.

West 54th Street became an enclave of the financially powerful. Among the Rockefellers' neighbors were Philip Lehman, head of Lehman Brothers, and James J. Goodwin, one of the principals of J. P. Morgan.

Five years later John D. Rockefeller purchased No. 13 from Mrs. Neilson and in 1909 he resold it to his son, who was still living there.

In the meantime James B. Dickson, president of the insurance firm Johnson & Higgins, and his wife, Harriet, had purchased the house next door in 1906. Mrs. Higgins would live on here for nearly half a century until her death on March 3, 1953.

John D. Rockefeller, Jr.
with his father in 1915.

In 1918, as World War I was drawing to an end, the Rockefellers moved across the street to 10 West 54th Street and the house at No. 13 was rented to businessman Howard Maxwell.

Eventually Maxwell moved permanently to his Glen Cove, Long Island, estate, "Maxwellton"; but the Rockefeller family retained possession of the house for three decades. Nelson, the son of John D. Rockefeller, Jr., used it for offices and for high-level business luncheons. Upon Harriet Higgins's death, Nelson purchased No. 15 and renovated it as the Museum of Primitive Art, which opened in 1957.

A passageway was carved into the rear of No. 13, connecting it to No. 22 West 55th Street where Nelson, now Governor of New York, maintained offices. It was in No. 13, in 1979, that Nelson Rockefeller died of a heart attack.

Shortly after Rockefeller's death, both houses were sold to Bernard H. Mendik.

Hardenbergh designed the houses as fraternal, rather than identical, twins.

Rockefeller's Museum of Primitive Art was closed in 1976 and its collection transferred to the Metropolitan Museum of Art. No. 13 was, until 2005, home to the Scandinavian restaurant Aquavit.

Today, the homes house offices and a restaurant, their charming outward appearances essentially unchanged since their completion in 1897.

FIFTH AVENUE

MORTON PLANT MANSION
FIFTH AVENUE
AND 52ND STREET

ST PATRICK'S CATHEDRAL
FIFTH AVENUE
50TH AND 51ST STREET

ST REGIS HOTEL,
FIFTH AVENUE AND 55TH STREET

THE HOUSE THAT A NECKLACE BOUGHT: THE MORTON PLANT MANSION

FIFTH AVENUE AND 52ND STREET

At the turn of the last century Fifth Avenue in midtown was known as "Millionaires' Row." Block after block of mansions, each attempting to outdo the other, lined the avenue from the 30s northward to Cornelius Vanderbilt's massive chateau at 57th Street. In 1902, following the demolition of the Roman Catholic Orphan Asylum, William K. Vanderbilt offered the corner lot at 52nd Street and Fifth Avenue for sale.

Morton F. Plant, the son of railroad tycoon Henry B. Plant, purchased the site, agreeing to Vanderbilt's stipulation that it could not be used for commercial purposes for twenty-five years.

Plant commissioned English-born architect Robert W. Gibson to design his residence. Construction would take three years to complete; but the results were dazzling. Gibson produced a marble and granite Italian Renaissance palace, one of the most elegant on the avenue.

With its entrance on 52nd Street, Plant's house turned its shoulder to the many Vanderbilt family houses that clustered around it. Over the doorway a stone balcony projected under a classic pediment. An ambitious stone balustrade surmounted the cornice, under which an ornate frieze was pierced by four-paned windows. The Plants established themselves as major players in the Fifth Avenue neighborhood.

In the meantime, things were changing downtown. The brownstone mansions of John Jacob and William Astor at Fifth Avenue and 34th Street had been replaced by the combined Waldorf and Astoria Hotels. Commerce was creeping up the avenue. By the time Morton and Nellie Plant moved into their new home, wealthy residents in the 30s were already beginning to abandon their homes to flee northward.

Morton was a yachtsman and owner of baseball teams in his spare time. He and his wife hosted elegant dinner parties and social events in the mansion until 1913. On August 8 of that year Nellie Plant, Morton's wife of twenty-six years, died. Shortly thereafter, the 61-year-old Plant met the 31-year-old Mae Caldwell Manwaring— wife of Selden B. Manwaring.

The Morton Plant house survives as the last truly
great mansion in Midtown.

In May of 1914, not ten months after the death of his wife, Plant announced his
engagement to Mae, who had obtained a divorce the previous month. A month later
the two were married at Plant's immense Groton, Connecticut, estate. Mae was,
reportedly, pleased with her wedding gift of $8 million.

By 1916 Morton and Mae (she preferred to be called Maisie) were concerned about
the stores and hotels that were inching closer and closer. Despite the restrictions in
his contract with Vanderbilt, Plant began building a French Renaissance palace at
Fifth Avenue and 86th Street, designed by Guy Lowell.

In the meantime Maisie Plant was window shopping. Pierre Cartier had opened a
New York branch of his Paris jewelry store and there she fell in love with a double-
stranded Oriental pearl necklace with a $1 million price tag (equal to about $16
million today).

An iron and stone fence surrounds the house. Cartier would later alter the street level with show windows and a Fifth Avenue entrance.

Before the advent of cultured pearls, flawless pearls were more valuable than diamonds. In Edwardian society a woman's social status was often measured by the length of her pearl ropes. Plant called on the jeweler and, in agreement with Vanderbilt, sold his Italian palazzo to Cartier for $100 and the necklace.

The *New York Times* reported, "Morton F. Plant, who is building his new city residence on upper Fifth Avenue . . . has sold his former home. It is one of the finest and newest of the expensive residences in what was, up to a few years ago, the choice Fifth Avenue residential locality, being opposite the Vanderbilt twin houses . . . Mr. Plant purchased his uptown plot at Eighty-sixth Street last year, as he felt that the business invasion had made too great an inroad in the old district below Fifty-ninth Street . . . ."

Cartier contracted William Welles Bosworth to convert the mansion into his new store. Bosworth's sympathetic transformation created a Fifth Avenue entrance, and show windows were seamlessly integrated into the façade. Much of the interior detailing and paneling, including the entire second-floor music room with its magnificent coffered ceiling, were preserved.

A year later, Morton Plant died. In 1919, Maisie married Colonel William Hayward. She married again in 1954, this time to the wealthy John E. Rovensky. Mae Caldwell Manwaring Plant Hayward Rovensky died in 1956 in the 86th Street mansion Morton Plant had built for her. Her double strand of Cartier pearls, once valued at over $1 million, was auctioned off for $150,000.

In 1970 the New York City Landmarks Preservation Commission designated the Plant Mansion a landmark.

THE 1901 BATTLE OVER FIFTH AVENUE: THE ST REGIS HOTEL

FIFTH AVENUE AND 55TH STREET

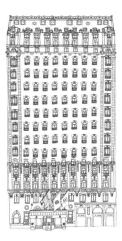

In 1901, John Jacob Astor, Jr., did what was unforgivable to many socially prominent New Yorkers. While three previous Astors had demolished their grand homes to erect exclusive hotels, they did so when the upper-class neighborhoods where they stood were becoming less fashionable.

This time John Jacob Astor, Jr., went too far. He purchased the mansions at the southeast corner of Fifth Avenue and 55th Street, demolished them, and began construction of the nineteen-story St. Regis Hotel, across the avenue from "Vanderbilt Row," the blocks of Vanderbilt family palaces. He betrayed his peers by contributing to the social crime of which New York's elite bitterly complained: encroachment of commerce into the exclusive Fifth Avenue mansion district.

Astor intended his hotel to be "as convenient and as luxurious as the most expensive private house in the city." That did not, however, appease the neighboring mansion owners.

The firm of Trowbridge & Livingston was hired to design the structure. The relatively young firm would go on to design important buildings such as the B. Altman Department Store on Fifth Avenue and J. P. Morgan's Wall Street headquarters; however, the St. Regis would be one of its most important early commissions. The architects opted for the trendy Beaux-Arts style that was sweeping the city and country.

The limestone-clad hotel would be festooned with garlands, balconies, French windows, and decorative wrought-iron railings. An elegant mansard roof, monumental console brackets, and snaking copper cresting added to the Parisian air of the design of a building intended to hold court over "the Queen of Avenues."

While the wealthy neighbors huddled over what to do about the intrusive structure rising in their midst, the Bureau of Buildings halted construction a year after the ground-breaking. The lush interiors of the hotel relied heavily on carved woodwork and expensive imported paneling. On May 14, 1902, Superintendent Stewart reported that the wood had not been properly fireproofed. "The doors and such wood stuffs are supposed to be thoroughly fireproofed," he said, "but they have not been…. I will not allow it, and will stop the work until they get the proper material, and replace what has already been put in."

In 1903 blasting of the solid rock for the 40-foot-deep foundation rattled the windowpanes of houses for blocks. Millionaires filed an injunction based on the depth of excavations. They were subsequently disappointed when Justice Clarke ruled in the hotel's favor.

By the spring of 1904, however, as construction was nearing completion, the neighbors devised another tactic. As the *New York Times* reported on May 13, "The new hotel is conceived and executed on a scale of sumptuosity quite without precedent. Naturally one of the first requisites of such a hotel is a license to sell liquor. It is evidently incapable of being sustained at that pitch of splendor upon a Crotonian basis."

The New York State liquor law clearly stated that the consent of the owners of two-thirds of the private property within 200 hundred feet of the establishment was required. It also stipulated that no license could be awarded to a business within 200 feet of a house of worship—and the rising St. Regis sat directly across from Fifth Avenue Presbyterian Church.

The *Times* said, "It is hardly to be supposed that the owners of the property affected, whether ecclesiastical or domestic, will acquiesce in a measure intended to make profitable what they unanimously regard as a nuisance. They must look upon the enterprising owner as guilty of 'incivism,' and it is not to be expected that they will be willing to condone proceedings so offensive to them…. Nobody can blame a householder whose residence is in what has heretofore been a fashionable residential district for objecting to an eighteen-story skyscraper across the way or around the corner. Such a structure necessarily injures the value of his property for the purposes for which he desires to maintain it."

Measurements were taken. The lawyers of the neighbors found that property line-to-property line the hotel fell within the 200-foot limit, constituting a violation of the state liquor law restrictions. The hotel, however, measured the distance from the main entrance of the hotel to the main entrance to the church, establishing a distance a few feet within the allowance. The authorities ruled in favor of the hotel and the license was awarded.

While the battle raged on, the hotel opened on September 4, 1904. The *Times*, intentionally or not, added fuel to the conflict saying, "The patronage which the management expects to attract is indicated by the locality in which it stands, the most exclusive residential section of the city."

The completed hotel cost an astonishing $5.5 million including furnishings. The Palm Room was illuminated by a skylight supported by marble arches and hung with antique tapestries. Seven crescent-shaped paintings were executed by artist Robert Van Vorst Sewell. Critic Helen Henderson split "decorative" and "illustrative" hairs.

She complained that while the paintings were "carefully finished" and "exquisitely drawn," they "defeat the purpose of decoration. They 'illustrate' the story of Cupid and Psyche."

A library contained 3,000 books. The two reception rooms, one paneled in white mahogany and the other in Circassian oak, were decorated with rare European antiques collected by the manager, R. M. Haan. The air throughout the hotel was filtered to remove dust and an electric plant and ice plant were housed in the basement.

"An idea of the decorative scheme of the St. Regis may be had from a description of the banquet hall. Here the walls are of paneled marble of a dull white color. The doors are painted to harmonize with the general

The newly completed hotel towered over the brownstone residences around it.

scheme, while the spaces between the doors and windows are covered with rich tapestries, the hangings being of yellow and white Venetian velvets," wrote the *Times*. Not one to accept defeat, William Rockefeller stood his ground by purchasing a new mansion nearby at 7 East 54th Street on October 17. "The purchase by Mr. Rockefeller is taken to mean that he and his neighbors have not given up their fight against the Hotel St. Regis liquor license, and it is intimated that effort may soon be made to have the license revoked on the ground that the necessary number of consents from adjoining property owners has not been obtained," said the *Times*.

John Jacob Astor responded by purchasing for $300,000 the home of James Everard at 697 Fifth Avenue adjoining the hotel to the south.

In the meantime a smear campaign was started against the hotel. A month after opening stories were sent to newspapers about a bomb exploding in the hotel's dining room, that guests were required to pay "per foot for filtered air," that a chocolate éclair cost "$500 per half portion," and "it is possible to live on oysters at $126 a day at the Hotel St. Regis." R. M. Haan complained that, "this sort of thing is a positive injury to my business."

Expensive Edwardian fashions were on display when dining at the St. Regis.

The bad press was reversed on December 1 when Prince Sadanaru Fushimi, the head of one of four royal families of Japan, arrived at the St. Regis for a two-week stay. The press covered the prince's every move and New York society, always impressed by titles, took notice. Four days after the prince's departure a dinner dance at the hotel in honor of Miss Corinne Robinson was announced by her parents. The debutante was a niece of President Roosevelt and the *New York Times* society page remarked that, "it will be the first large fashionable affair given at the new hotel which may now compete with the Waldorf-Astoria, Sherry's and Delmonico's for patronage of this kind. Miss Alice Roosevelt, who has been in town for a week, will be present."

Within the month it was announced that "Mr. and Mrs. I. Townsend Burden and Miss Gwendolyn Burden, who returned from abroad recently, are at the St. Regis. Mr. and Mrs. William K. Vanderbilt, Jr., will also make that hotel their Winter headquarters, and Mr. and Mrs. Oliver H. P. Belmont may be there also."

The St. Regis had arrived.

In April of the next year William Rockefeller realized that while he had money, John Jacob Astor had friends. Senator Saxe, acting on behalf of Senator Elsberg, introduced a bill "for the protection of the respectable hotels." The bill provided that the section of the liquor law restricting an establishment to be more than 200 feet from a house of worship and to require two-thirds assent of neighbors within the same area "shall not apply to hotels that have 200 rooms above the basement used for the accommodation of guests." Lawmakers were quite blunt that the new law applied specifically to the St. Regis.

John Jacob Astor had won his war.

On April 15, 1912, Astor died aboard the *Titanic* and his son, Vincent Astor, took over ownership of the St. Regis and its sister hotel, the Knickerbocker on 42nd Street. Eight years later, Prohibition swept the country, dealing a serious blow to the hotel industry. Astor closed the King Cole Bar in the Knickerbocker, removing to storage the famous 30-foot-long 1906 mural by Maxfield Parrish, *King Cole and His Fiddlers Three*.

As hard times continued, Astor sold the St. Regis to the Durham Realty Corporation in February of 1927. The company, owned by the Duke family, remodeled the rooms, had architects Sloan & Robertson create an addition on East 55th Street, and relied on the hotel's reputation as a marketing tool, calling it "fundamentally part of Fifth Avenue."

In 1935, after having been on loan to the New York Racquet Club on Park Avenue, the Maxfield Parrish mural was reinstalled in the St. Regis. Helen Henderson again chimed in. "That quaintly humorous panel," she instructed, "delightful as it is, is illustration rather than decoration."

The newly renovated Art Deco dining room, called The King Cole Room, became one of New York's most elite dining destinations, and remained so for decades.

The elegant entrance welcomes guests more than a century after the battle over Fifth Avenue.

By the mid-1960s the hotel was in genuine danger of demolition. The owners leased it in February 1966 to the Sheraton Corporation of America, raising the eyebrows of New Yorkers who considered that the idea of a chain managing the beloved hotel was a sort of sacrilege.

Sheraton reacted with a reassuring marketing release a year later. "While maintaining all the fine traditions for which The St. Regis has always been renowned, Sheraton has lavished a king's ransom renewing its gilt-edged elegance. Expensive furnishings have been brought from France, in the fashion that found favor with two of France's greatest monarchs. Rich carpets from the Middle East. Multi-faceted crystal chandeliers from Sweden. Ah, yes, the kings would be at home here. They would nod approval at the courtly service and the magician-like resourcefulness of the concierge. They would dine royally in a choice of restaurants respected for their *grande cuisine* and loved for their light-hearted sophistication."

Nevertheless, the striking King Cole Room was remodeled and the mural moved to a much smaller barroom renamed The King Cole Bar. In 2005 renovation began to covert 59 of the hotel rooms to 33 condominium apartments with prices ranging from $1.6 to $7.2 million.

Despite the changes to the grand hotel, it remains an important and cherished fixture on midtown Fifth Avenue, what the New York City Landmarks Commission called "one of the most elegant and sophisticated Beaux-Arts style buildings in New York."

ST. PATRICK'S CATHEDRAL
FIFTH AVENUE AT 50TH AND 51ST STREETS

James Renwick, Jr., was 25 years old when he received the commission to design Grace Church in 1843. An engineer, he had no training as an architect and had, to date, designed only a fountain at Bowling Green in southern Manhattan. Renwick did not disappoint, however. Completed in 1846, Grace Church was a masterpiece —and among the very first major Gothic Revival structures in the nation.

Within the year he had designed the Smithsonian Institution Building, often referred to as the Renwick Castle. The architect would, for the rest of his life, be a busy man. But he would hold none of his designs in greater importance than the masterful St. Patrick's Cathedral.

The white marble cathedral is a masterpiece in Gothic Revival architecture.

The first Archbishop of New York, John Hughes, summoned Renwick in 1853 to start plans for a replacement to the cathedral on Mott Street, which had been completed in 1815. Although the existing St. Patrick's Cathedral was the largest church in the city, the Archbishop yearned for a more magnificent church.

The land Hughes had selected for the site, on Fifth Avenue between 50th and 51st Streets, was well north of the established city, resulting in its being deemed by skeptics as "Hughes's Folly." Renwick went to work on the drawings; according to Archbishop John Murphy Farley's 1908 history of the cathedral, they "were changed several times until 1858, when they were definitely agreed upon."

With the plans approved, the Archbishop presented Renwick and his assisting architect, William Rodrigue (who coincidentally or not married Hughes's sister Margaret), with contracts. Each would receive $2,500 a year for eight years and the Archbishop had the right to suspend or discontinue the building at will. It was a highly unusual arrangement, although financially advantageous for Renwick and Rodrigue.

The plans that were "definitely agreed upon" were for a soaring, white marble Gothic Revival structure that would compete with the great medieval structures of Europe. The cost of construction was fixed with the Hall and Joyce Company, the builders, at $850,000, and a contract was signed on March

Harper's Weekly featured Archbishop Hughes's funeral in the unfinished Cathedral in 1864.

5, 1859, with the stipulation that the construction would be finished on or before January 1, 1867.

The cornerstone had been laid on August 15, 1858, half a year before the contracts were finalized. The immense structure rose steadily, filling the Fifth Avenue block towards Madison Avenue. Then in 1861 the Civil War broke out. As the conflict worsened, more and more of the men of New York abandoned their jobs to fight for the Union. Eventually work on the cathedral stopped.

Archbishop Hughes would not live to see his magnificent cathedral rise above Fifth Avenue. He died in 1864, succeeded by Bishop John McCloskey, who would take up the project as construction commenced again after the war. Two decades after it was begun, St. Patrick's Cathedral was dedicated on May 25, 1879.

The new cathedral had a seating capacity of 18,000, and every seat was filled at 10:00 a.m. when McCloskey, by now a Cardinal, and an entourage of bishops and priests proceeded up the aisle. A large force of policemen was positioned around the building to keep order. A local newspaper described it as "the noblest temple ever raised in any land to the memory of Saint Patrick," and as "the glory of Catholic America."

The cathedral was the scene of a major scare when, on St. Patrick's Day 1918, a crowd of thousands was assembled awaiting the parade. Everyone remembered the bomb that had been discovered in the church on March 2, 1915, and anarchism was a constant threat. Suddenly the throng was panicked by an enormous chunk of a stone spire that broke loose. The largest piece crashed through the roof, breaking through the organ loft inside. Outside, large stone fragments showered down on the masses.

"The crash and roar of the big missile caused fear that the whole great structure had been dynamited and might topple into the street," reported the *New York Times*. As the dignitaries in the reviewing stand stampeded to get away, Congressman Thomas F. Smith was knocked to the ground and suffered a broken wrist.

The 1915 bomb would not be the last of the threats to the cathedral. In January 1951 a letter was received announcing that a bomb would be set off at a Sunday mass. And between December 1951 and July 1952 there would be five more bomb threats. On July 12, a deep-voiced male telephoned the Rev. Edward Connors, ordering him to "get them out," referring to worshippers in the cathedral. Thirty minutes later he phoned again, warning "your beautiful cathedral will be blown up before midnight."

St. Patrick's Cathedral remains a work in progress. In 1927 Cardinal Hayes initiated an ambitious $2 million renovation project that included an enlarged sanctuary, a rebuilt choir gallery, new organs in the gallery and chancel, new nave flooring and pews, and a new baptistery. Hayes also commissioned the great bronze doors, which, it was reported, he felt were more "in keeping with the rest of the building." Seventeen of the nineteen altars, as well as the Stations of the Cross, were repaired, cleaned, and repolished.

Work was done on the cathedral throughout the 1940s. Cardinal Spellman added new upper windows, a new high altar, a replacement altar in the Lady Chapel, and extensive exterior stone restoration.

Restoration of the entire interior was done in 1972; the exterior was restored in 1979; and in 1984 a six-year structural repair process was begun. This included replacement of much of the roof, resetting of the exterior steps, refinishing the doors, restoring the bells, and rebuilding the organs. In 2013 through 2014 the cathedral was once again shrouded in scaffolding and construction netting.

Throughout the years the cathedral has been the focal point of protestors railing against the Vietnam War, the discontinuing of the Latin mass, and, annually, the exclusion of gay groups from the St. Patrick's Day parade.

Despite Helen Henderson's criticisms of the great cathedral, the New York Landmarks Preservation Commission considered that "St. Patrick's Cathedral represents the epitome of the Gothic Revival in New York City" and called it, "A marvel of architectural design for its day."

PARK AVENUE

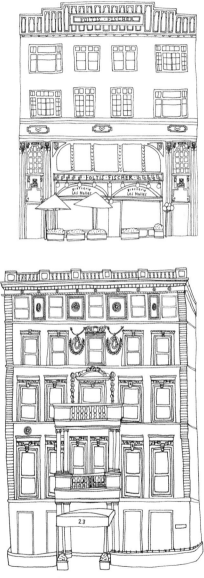

THE 1929
FOLTIS-FISCHER
BUILDING
411-13 PARK AVENUE SOUTH

ADELAIDE DOUGLAS HOUSE,
57 PARK AVENUE

THE J. HAMPDEN ROBB HOUSE,
23 PARK AVENUE

FOLTIS-FISCHER BUILDING

411–413 PARK AVENUE SOUTH

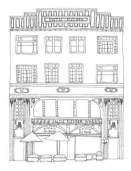

In 1909 at the age of 19, Constantine Foltis immigrated to New York and found a job with the Childs restaurant chain. By 1928 he owned several stores, known as the Foltis Food Shops, which focused on healthful produce and meats.

The 1920s saw the rise in popularity of a new concept in dining—the self-service restaurant. Chains like Horn & Hardart provided shop girls and businessmen quick, inexpensive meals in clean and attractive environments. Constantine Foltis got in on the act.

On December 13, 1928, he consolidated his stores with another small chain of shops along with an assortment of restaurants, creating the Foltis-Fischer self-service restaurants. *Moody's Industrial Manual* recorded that he acquired "chains of restaurants formerly operated as Foltis Food Shops and the Fischer Food Shops and 15 independent restaurants, making a total of 29 restaurants acquired."

Foltis continued to expand. Within the year he announced in the *New York Times* a planned restaurant at 411–13 Fourth Avenue (later renamed Park Avenue South). On September 11, 1929, the newspaper reported that "following alterations of the present property, they will open their thirty-first restaurant."

On the site was a four-story building that housed the O.L. Cushman Co. lunchroom. On the second floor were offices and the top two floors held "non-housekeeping apartments," as recorded in Department of Buildings records. Foltis commissioned Erhard Djorup to renovate the existing structure.

The Austrian-born architect had been busy as a partner in Bark & Djorup designing Art Deco office buildings such as the massive 1384 Broadway, completed in 1928 for developer Abraham Lefcourt. But that same year the partnership fell apart, and the Foltis-Fischer restaurant was apparently one of Djorup's first independent commissions after the split.

Djorup brought the old building squarely into the Jazz Age. A two-story base of black stone was highlighted with white Art Deco decorations at the second floor and gold at the first. A frieze within the central double-height arch announced the restaurant's name. On either side stair-stepped openings at both levels were flanked by streamlined pilasters. The upper floors, clad in white terra-cotta, were decidedly less decorated. Above it all, an Art Deco parapet also advertised the Foltis-Fischer name.

The renovations were completed in May 1930. The sidewalk level housed the restaurant, the second floor was used as offices, and the third and fourth floors were, again, rented as residential space.

Foltis continued to market his restaurant as serving wholesome foods. The timing of his ambitious venture, however, was unfortunate. As the building at 411–13 Fourth Avenue was being renovated, the Stock Market Crash plunged the nation into the Great Depression. It was also a time of labor unrest and the bullying of small businesses by organized crime.

The fonts on a matchbook cover carry on the modern motif of the restaurant's façade.

Trouble started for the restaurants when, in July 1932, underworld boss Arthur Flegenheimer (known in mob circles as Dutch Schultz) and his gang organized the Metropolitan Restaurant and Cafeteria Association. The Association took control of two unions "by threats, violence and corruption," according to district attorneys later, and restaurant employees were forced to join.

Restaurant owners, including Foltis-Fischer, were convinced to join the association "by threats and actual throwing of stench bombs, beatings and other violence, intimidation of customers and employees, and placing picket lines where there were no strikes," reported the *New York Times*. The Association was collecting $5,500 a week in "membership dues."

By October 31, 1936, when the Schultz gang was indicted on charges of extortion, attempted extortion, and conspiracy in the $2 million-a-year racket, the Foltis-Fischer restaurants had paid out $9,975 in protection money—almost $150,000 today.

Despite the restaurant's paying its "dues," in 1933 workers in the Foltis-Fischer chain went on strike. In May that year Dorothy Day, writing in the *Catholic Worker*, opined, "For generally bad working conditions, Foltis-Fischer is one of the worst restaurants in New York. You will notice that men are picketing up and down in front of their chain of restaurants throughout the city, and the strike of employees there has been a bitter one." She added, "If the public cooperated with the workers and refused to go into a restaurant where men were picketing in front, there might be more chance for strikers to win their fight for justice."

The same year that workers were picketing in front of 411–13 Fourth Avenue, Adolf Hitler became Chancellor of Germany. Within a month the German Reichstag was burned to the ground and two weeks later the first concentration camp, Oranienburg, was opened. By the end of 1933 Hitler had full dictatorial power and Germany had withdrawn from the League of Nations.

It would be years before the United States was pulled into a world conflict; but the Foltis-Fischer Co. chain took an early and symbolic stand. On May 8, 1934, it was announced, "That thousands of New Yorkers heretofore using the German yeast product, Savita, will do without it, became known yesterday as the Foltis Fischer Corporation restaurants and retail shops prepared to ban this and other German imports."

The Depression, the mob, and labor problems all took their toll. In 1938 the company declared bankruptcy after a decade of doing business. In 1944 the Emigrant Industrial Savings Bank sold the building to the 411 Fourth Avenue Realty Corporation.

Throughout the remainder of the century, the structure remained unchanged— offices and a showroom on the ground floor, offices on the second, and four apartments per floor above. Most remarkable is that the wonderful Art Deco façade remained, for the most part, untouched.

In 1990 the ground floor became a restaurant once again. Les Halles Boucherie Rotisserie is still in the space today; and astonishingly, after nearly a century, the bold zigzagged frieze still advertises Foltis-Fischer.

The remarkable Art Deco facade survives almost totally intact.

ADELAIDE TOWNSEND DOUGLAS HOUSE

57 PARK AVENUE

In March 1902, when excavation for the Park Avenue subway resulted in a calamitous cave-in that seriously damaged several mansions, a scandal was being quietly ignored by New York society. As the clean-up on Park Avenue began, Mrs. William P. Douglas and her daughter, Edith Sybil, were anticipating an ocean voyage as guests of J. P. Morgan on his yacht, the *Corsair.*

Adelaide Townsend Douglas was married to capitalist William Proctor Douglas. Although he had been a member of the first American international polo team, he was best known as a yachtsman. In 1871 he successfully defended the America's Cup with his schooner *Sappho.* But since 1895, according to Jean Strouse's *Morgan: American Financier,* Adelaide had been carrying on an affair with Morgan.

Rumors of Morgan and Adelaide's affair never rose above a whisper. William Douglas moved out of their home on East 46th Street in 1903. In 1908, after son J. Gordon Douglas married, William moved again, this time to 12 West 76th Street and, finally, the *Social Register* listed him and Adelaide separately.

Meanwhile, John J. Murphy had sold his mansion at 57 Park Avenue just weeks following the cave-in. The *New York Times* reported that it was "one of the houses which was badly damaged" and described it as "four stories in height.... It is understood that before the cave-in Mr. Murphy held the property at $65,000." (That valuation would translate to over $1 million today.)

Now, in 1909 with only Sybil left at home, Adelaide laid plans for a new home— one just steps from the J. P. Morgan mansion at Madison Avenue and 37th Street. On April 8, 1909, the *Times* reported that, "Architect Horace Trumbauer of Philadelphia has filed plans for the new six-story residence to be built by Mrs. Adelaide L. Douglas at 57 Park Avenue. It is to be 25.1 feet front, with a façade of granite and limestone, and will cost $120,000." It is interesting to note that by now, although she was not divorced, the newspapers referred to Adelaide by her own name and not her husband's.

The unlivable mansion of John Murphy had been purchased in a settlement by the Interboro Rapid Transit Company. Now it was razed to be replaced by an elegant and restrained townhouse in the French Classic style of Louis XVI. Apparently

Adelaide did not need to worry about the high cost of the structure—her grandson later reported that Morgan financed it; and nearly half a century later the *New York Times* brashly announced that it was "originally built for J. P. Morgan."

Construction went on for two years and in 1911 it was completed. Trumbauer managed to ornament the house with exquisite bas-relief

Close inspection reveals the quality craftsmanship in the spandrel carvings.

carvings, French ironwork, and a full menu of window shapes and dimensions, all the while maintaining calm and elegance.

Guests entered into a marble-lined reception hall. On the first floor was the sumptuous dining room. Above, where tall French doors opened onto the Park Avenue balcony, were two salons decorated in the French eighteenth-century style. Adelaide's bedroom was on the third floor, facing the rear, along with the library to the front.

The one guest who did not enter through the double entrance doors on Park Avenue was J. P. Morgan. According to family members, the millionaire had a private entrance at the rear of the house.

If New York society rebuffed those involved in extramarital affairs, it made an exception for the fabulously wealthy. Dinner parties in the Park Avenue house were regularly noted in the society pages—and attended.

Adelaide was alone in the mansion following her daughter's marriage. Edith—referred to as Sybil by friends—was married on January 27, 1913, in fashionable St. George's Chapel. She was wed to William Fitzhugh Whitehouse. Although the *Sun* cautioned that "only relatives and a few intimate friends will witness the ceremony," those who attended the wedding included society's elite. The *Times* listed both Mrs. Cornelius Vanderbilt and another "Mrs. Vanderbilt," Colonel and Mrs. William Jay, Mr. and Mrs. Ernest Iselin, Mr. and Mrs. Lewis Iselin, and Alfonso de Navarro among others.

Following the ceremony, Park Avenue was lined with smart vehicles and waiting drivers as Adelaide hosted the reception in the house.

On June 3, 1919, Adelaide's husband died in his home at 12 West 76th Street at the age of 77. Her relationship with William Douglas had apparently remained cordial. When the will was read, Adelaide received $50,000 of the over $1 million estate and one third of the income from her husband's real estate.

Adelaide continued the expected schedule of a wealthy New York socialite. Each summer her Newport estate, "Cozy Nook," was opened and every fall it was closed. In front of No. 57 Park Avenue, horse-drawn carriages gave way to shining limousines that dropped guests off for dinner parties and receptions.

Adelaide made the change as well. In 1932 her chauffeur was 22-year-old Servie Laccesaglio who, with other staff, lived in the house. But apparently Laccesaglio felt his Depression Era wages and free board were not enough to see him through.

Early on the morning of December 30, 1932, the chauffeur and two other men noticed Brooklyn restaurant owner Max Advocate emerging from the 20th Avenue subway station in Brooklyn on his way home. The men forced him into their automobile, drove him several miles, then robbed him of $150 in cash, a $25 check, and his bank book.

A passerby had seen the abduction, noted the license plate, and notified the police. Unfortunately for Laccesaglio and his accomplices, the New York Police Department had recently installed radios in its patrol cars. The *New York Times* credited the technological innovation with their arrests. "The police radio system early this morning snared three men half an hour after they had released a Brooklyn restaurant proprietor," it said.

Adelaide Douglas's young chauffeur learned that crime does not pay—and presumably lost a job and a free room.

Three years later, on October 23, 1935, the colorful 83-year-old Adelaide Townsend Douglas died in her Park Avenue mansion. Ironically, her *New York Times* obituary related more about her husband's life and accomplishments than it did about her.

The Douglas mansion sat vacant for a period, then was leased by Arthur Charn in June 1937. Before long, however, the house would be converted to high-end apartments. Here in 1940 Maurice and Martha Speiser lived. The couple auctioned off their extensive art collection in 1944 at the Parke-Bernet Galleries. Included were 115 canvases by Picasso, Chagall, Matisse, and other masters; fifteen sculptures by artists including Epstein and Brancusi; and 761 books on modern art. Among the masterworks sold were Modigliani's *Garçon a la Veste Bleu* and Utrillo's *Eglise Sainte Marguerite*.

In 1942 the Douglas Estate sold the house built for Adelaide. For a few years it housed the offices of American British Technology and the Welfare League for Retarded Children. Then on June 17, 1959, the United States Olympic Association announced that "shortly we will have a new home." The organization, which had been operating from the Hotel Biltmore, purchased the house at 57 Park Avenue.

The Olympic Association remained in the Douglas mansion for nearly two decades. In 1979 what was now referred to as the "Olympic House" was sold for $5 million to the Government of Guatemala as its Mission to the United Nations. As the Landmarks Preservation Commission remarked the following year, "Despite changes to the interior of the house, the exterior remains almost entirely intact. As such it is a reminder of the period before World War I when Park Avenue was an elegant residential thoroughfare."

The lavish townhouse of Adelaide Douglas is one of the last remnants of lower Park Avenue's fashionable residential days.

J. HAMPDEN ROBB HOUSE
23 PARK AVENUE

By the time James Hampden Robb commissioned Stanford White to design his home at 23 Park Avenue, he had already been a cotton broker, a New York State Assemblyman, and a State Senator. At the time, in 1888, he was busy with the functions of his post as Commissioner of the Parks Department.

Park Avenue and the streets leading off it were lined with substantial brownstone homes of a decade earlier. White's design for the Robb mansion would be strikingly different. He created a five-story Renaissance-inspired palazzo of iron spot brick with exuberant terra-cotta trim on a high brownstone base.

The pillared entrance portico was mimicked in the stone balcony directly above. A finely crafted cast-iron balcony and two-story oriel window on the south side added to the visual appeal.

Although the mansion was essentially completed in 1891, it would be another two years before the beautiful interiors were ready. Stanford White put four of the most respected interior decorating firms of the period—L. Marcotte & Co.; Joseph Cabus; Pottier, Stymus & Co.; and Herter Brothers—to work inside the house.

Robb and his wife, Cornelia Van Rensselaer Thayer Robb, moved into their newly completed home in 1893. Below imported, historic ceilings, the couple filled the rooms with rare art and antiques, sixteenth-century Persian rugs, Gobelins tapestries, and paintings by Rubens, Van Dyke, and Emmanuel.

While Robb was aggressively involved in the Democratic Party, he invested equal passion into his Parks position. He steadfastly refused to allow any incursion of commerce onto park property set aside for public recreation. "Only by eternal vigilance can the parks be maintained and developed as they ought to be, for there is never a time when someone is not trying to 'work' something to his own personal advantage and to the detriment of the public," he said.

During his Senate years he had fought for the appropriation to establish the State reservation of Niagara Falls, speaking fervently of "the preservation of the beauties and the breathing places of the State." When he was offered the position of Assistant Secretary of State by President Grover Cleveland, Robb politely declined.

In 1891 the Robb mansion sat among wide brownstone residences of a generation earlier.

Cornelia Robb was often of frail health. Ten years after the couple moved into the Park Avenue mansion, she died. Thereafter daughter Cornelia Van Rensselaer Robb, called Nellie by her friends and family, acted as hostess of the house.

J. Hampden Robb died in the house on January 21, 1911. Cornelia remained in the house for another year, then sold most of the furnishings at a highly publicized auction at the Plaza Hotel in April of 1912.

Among the items sold were a 7-by-12-foot Persian carpet that brought $22,000 (about three quarters of a million today) and a sixteenth-century terra-cotta *Madonna and Child* purchased by the Metropolitan Museum of Art.

On Robb's death the mansion had been inherited by his grandson, J. Hampden Robb II. By now Park Avenue was changing. One by one the grand mansions were falling, to be replaced by office buildings. In 1913 Robb leased the magnificent Italian mansion to Jane E. Patterson, who converted it to a boarding house. Patterson had walls erected and plumbing fixtures installed to adapt the dwelling for its new purpose.

Were it not for the Advertising Club of New York, the Robb House, would eventually have been demolished. The organization acquired the house in 1923 as its clubhouse, and architect Fred F. French was hired to renovate it for the club's purposes. A local clergyman made a plea to the club's membership: "Save as much of White as possible. He had a wonderful sense of proportion. There is something about a house where he had a free hand that gives you a special feeling of comfort. That's why I say… that I would rather have a Stanford White house than a painting by Rembrandt."

Renovations were completed within the year, at a cost of $250,000, and the club opened on January 6, 1924. Heeding the appeal of the minister, French kept much of White's interiors intact.

The clubhouse was enlarged after a fire damaged the structure in 1946. The house abutting to the rear, at 103 East 35th Street, was incorporated as an extension of the Robb mansion. Here, two years later, Mrs. Franklin D. Roosevelt gave an impassioned plea for help for delinquent boys.

The house, considered by many to be one of Stanford White's finest residential designs, was converted to co-op apartments in 1977. Although landmark status was not designated until 1998, the

The mansion is considered by many to be one of Stanford White's masterpieces.

conversion left the exterior untouched, as well as many of the surviving interior details.

The magnificent Stanford White Robb mansion still stands regally at its Park Avenue corner, a reminder of a time when the homes of many of Manhattan's millionaires lined the then-residential thoroughfare.

CENTRAL PARK

SEVENTH REGIMENT NEW YORK
ONE HUNDRED AND SEVENTH UNITED STATES INFANTRY
1917 IN MEMORIAM 1918

107TH INFANTRY MEMORIAL, AT EAST 65TH STREET

THE INDIAN HUNTER

CENTRAL PARK

CAROUSEL

107TH INFANTRY MEMORIAL

CENTRAL PARK AT EAST 65TH STREET

SEVENTH REGIMENT NEW YORK
ONE HUNDRED AND SEVENTH UNITED STATES INFANTRY
1917 IN MEMORIAM 1918

Tensions between the British and Americans did not abruptly end after the American Revolution. In 1806 the British warships were back. They sailed into New York Bay, claiming the lawful right to seize and search all American vessels and remove British subjects.

The invasion incited New York's citizens, and in response the Seventh Regiment of New York was organized as a state defense force. The regiment would be called into action again six years later in the War of 1812. But decades on the face of the unit changed with the Astor Place Riots in 1849.

Twenty thousand working-class demonstrators mobbed the elite residential neighborhood around the Astor Place Opera House. The group was ostensibly protesting against a British actor appearing there, but the disturbance quickly turned against the upper class in general. The mansions of some of New York's wealthiest citizens were pummeled with bricks and rocks, breaking windows and causing panic.

The Seventh Regiment responded, firing into the crowd and driving away what *Harper's Bazaar* called "the bleeding rioters, demoralized and defeated." The bloody confrontation left more than 25 dead and 120 wounded. The grateful upper-class residents did not forget their champions and the regiment became its favorite. The sons of the wealthy enlisted in the force over the years, earning the group its nicknames, "The Silk Stocking Regiment" and "The Dandy 7th."

Following the Civil War a statue was erected in Central Park called *The Citizen Soldier*. Sculpted by John Quincy Adams Ward, it depicted a Seventh Regiment soldier staring thoughtfully into the distance. It would not be the last tribute to the regiment in the park.

The regiment built a new armory in the 1870s on Park Avenue—a magnificent structure as much clubhouse as arsenal—with interiors by the premier designers of the day including Louis C. Tiffany and Herter Brothers. It was the only armory in the United States constructed wholly with private funds.

On Wednesday, June 28, 1916, the *New York Tribune* published photographs of the regiment marching up Eleventh Avenue in straight ranks and files, their rifles

The grouping is seemingly alive with motion as the figures
appear to burst forth from Central Park.

on their shoulders, heading to the train depot. Smiling men in doughboy hats were
pictured kissing their children goodbye and waving jubilantly from the rear platform
of a railroad car. Among the excited volunteers was young art student Karl Illava.
They were off to secure the Mexican border after Pancho Villa burned New Mexico
army barracks and robbed stores.

It would not be many more months before the smiles were gone from the faces of
the Seventh Regiment. In April 1917 the United States was pulled into the ghastly
World War in Europe. The Seventh Regiment, renamed the 107th Infantry, shipped
off to serve its country, with General O'Ryan's 27th Division. The regiment would
now have participated in every war since the Revolution.

Karl Illava rose to the rank of Sergeant Major while overseas. Before long,
the photographs appearing in the *Tribune* were not of smiling soldiers, but of
those lost in combat. In September 1918 the 107th was part of the assault on the
Hindenburg Line, Germany's intricate line of defense in northeast France. The
assault was successful, with four of the unit's members earning the Congressional
Medal of Honor—one posthumously. For victory came at a steep price, with the
Dandy 7th suffering 60 percent casualties. The fresh young men who marched
off to war from their posh Park Avenue armory would come home much older
and much changed.

All of New York City turned out to cheer the returning heroes. On March 25,
1919, the *New-York Tribune* remarked that for New Yorkers, the new designation

of the 107th Infantry did not matter. "It was still the old 7th, the 'Dandy 7th,' that marched up Fifth Avenue yesterday."

Thousands waved flags and cheered themselves hoarse. There were receptions and speeches. But when someone asked a private, "What are the boys going to do tonight?" he answered, "I guess when they all get inside they'll drop that pack and rifle and say 'Thank God!' and go to bed."

Sergeant Major Karl Illava was no longer the naive art student who had left New York in 1917. Almost immediately, he was given his first commission, a statue to commemorate the 27th and 30th Divisions, to be erected at Spartanburg, South Carolina. The sculpture was less heroic than realistic. It was war seen through the eyes of a soldier.

The *Touchstone* commented on the statue as Illava was still at work. "Two changes are apparent in student art as the soldiers return from The War with their eyes still only half-seeing after the glare of the too-close vision of battlefields," it said. "The soldier-student has become poised. He suddenly found himself in the turmoil that tore nations, and he grew old, as it were, in a day. When he speaks it is as though he possessed the wisdom of years of suffering; and we are forced to listen with respect. The soldier-student has also learned to see more minutely. He has learned that the task to be well-done must be done to the smallest detail. He does not forget, his military training has taught him that his life depended upon his memory."

Karl Illava's attention to the smallest detail and his acute memory of the horrors that he and his fellow soldiers in the 7th Regiment endured would be called upon again. In 1924 a group was formed, the 7th–107th Memorial Committee, to erect a memorial to the brave doughboys who fought, some to their deaths, defending their nation. Karl Illava was given the responsibility to depict his own regiment in action.

Perhaps the memories of war were too close to the surface for Illava's comrades; for the models he used were businessmen and other civilians. Paul Cornell, head of an advertising agency, would be his central figure—chosen, according to the artist, because he represented "a typical American." The *Princeton Alumni Weekly* reported that "The figures on either side of Mr. Cornell—figures representing the brute in war—are Kenneth Logan, a Scarsdale realtor, and Mr. Ollin J. Coit, big-game hunter and friend of the late Theodore Roosevelt." The magazine listed the other posers, adding, "None of the men in the group was in the 107th Infantry Regiment, which the statue commemorates but several of them saw military service."

Models aside, what resulted was dramatic and gripping. Illava's firsthand experience with the terrors of war burst forth in his depiction of the group of seven soldiers in the attack on the Western Front. The sculptor masterfully captured fear, determination, and valor in the faces of the young men facing death in battle. Three hold outstretched bayonets as one holds a dying companion in his arms. The feet of the soldiers are immersed in a boiling, swirling mass of bronze reflective of the chaos of war.

Illava surrounded the soldiers' feet with swirling bronze—symbolic of the chaos of war.

The completed statue was dedicated on September 29, 1927. It sits upon a 25-foot-wide stepped granite base designed by architects Rogers and Haneman at the end of East 67th Street at Fifth Avenue. The powerful grouping seems to advance from the thicket of Central Park, bursting forth onto the avenue.

The commanding memorial, surely the masterwork of the young veteran sculptor, was called by Cal Snyder in his book *Out of Fire and Valor*, "A doughboy sculpture to end all others."

JOHN WARD'S
THE INDIAN HUNTER
CENTRAL PARK

The ancestors of John Quincy Adams Ward landed in Jamestown, Virginia, in 1607. As years passed, one group moved westward, stopping in the rural area of Urbana, Ohio. There on a farm on June 29, 1830, Ward was born.

Ward's father was an ardent Whig and "enthusiastic admirer of Andrew Jackson's greatest political enemy," as the *New York Times* would later explain. These political leanings were the origin of Ward's somewhat ungainly name.

Ward had a strong artistic bent and spent his leisure time attempting to create clay figures. *The Times* said, "He never saw a piece of sculpture before he was fifteen years old, but long before that he had learned how to make such odd figures with mud and clay that the country people called him 'Ward's queer boy.'" Although his parents considered his hobby "foolishness," his older sister recognized his potential.

She convinced the Wards to allow her to take young John to live with her in New York, using his frail health as her excuse. He entered the studio of Brooklyn sculptor Henry Kirke Brown in 1849 as a student and assistant, most notably working on Brown's equestrian statue of George Washington for Union Square.

While John Quincy Adams Ward was learning about sculpture, the mood towards American art was changing. Although aspiring artists still sailed off to Paris and Rome for formal training, there was a growing interest at home in truly American art created by American artists, and Ward wanted to be part of it. With no interest in studying abroad, he proclaimed that "we shall never have good art at home until our best artists reside here."

Toward the end of the seven years he worked with Browne, he created his first sketch of a Native American hunting with his dog. In 1859, the year after Frederick Law Olmsted and Calvert Vaux began work on the new Central Park, his sketch had progressed to a plaster model which he exhibited at the Washington Art Club and the Pennsylvania Academy of the Fine Arts.

In 1861 he established a studio at Nos. 7 and 9 West 49th Street and reworked his *Indian Hunter*. A year later a bronze statuette was exhibited at the National Academy of Design's annual exhibition.

The natural posture of the figures was in sharp contrast to the formal statuary Victorians were accustomed to.

Unsure that his work was faithful to his subject, Ward traveled to frontier posts in the Dakotas in 1864 to study Native Americans. Here, according to *The Times*, "the Indian, not yet sophisticated out of his character by cheap clothing, was still to be seen at his ancestral pursuits. This lithe, sinewy, crouching, watchful creature had nothing in common with the 'classical' athlete."

Upon his return, Ward reworked the *Indian Hunter* once again, making the hunter's hair shaggier, raising his arm holding the bow, and refining the facial features. In the autumn of the following year a larger than life-size plaster sculpture was exhibited in Snedecor's gallery on lower Broadway. The *New York Times* said, "It was a new type of sculpture because it was the result of a faithful study of a type in life."

The statue would change the life of John Quincy Adams Ward.

The new statue was illustrated in the Manual of the Corporation of the City of New York in 1869.

Ward later told the newspaper, "It attracted some attention, and it had not been there very long before a visitor appeared in my studio, announced himself as August Belmont, explained that he had been interested in my work, and then gave me an order for a statue of Commodore Perry. From that day to this I have never been without a commission."

August Belmont was not the only moneyed citizen to notice the work. A group of wealthy New Yorkers including Cyrus Butler, Robert Hoe, Le Grand Lockwood, H. Pierpont Morgan, and H. G. Marquand established the "Indian Hunter Fund" to finance Ward's bronze casting of the statue and to push for its inclusion in the developing Central Park. The completed sculpture was shipped to France, to be exhibited in the Paris Exhibition. On July 4, 1867, the *New-York Tribune* noted that the work was one of three American sculptures in the fair: "Ward's 'Indian Hunter,' and Thompson's Napoleon are appreciated here," the article said, "as they deserve to be; and I have not yet discovered any sculpture which surpasses them in the union of originality with a truly antique largeness and simplicity."

Ward's *Indian Hunter* was ground-breaking in its naturalism—a u-turn from the Neoclassical style. Half a century later, art critic Charles Henry Caffin would call attention to its "absence of any preconceived theories of technique, so that the group has something of a primitive, almost barbarous feeling; which, however, seems strangely appropriate to the subject." Most important, it was an American statue of a uniquely American subject.

Upon the sculpture's return to New York, it was presented to Andrew H. Green, Comptroller of Central Park, on December 28, 1868, by the Committee of the Indian Hunter Fund. In its contributory letter, the group said, "We have peculiar satisfaction in placing at your disposal a work so truly American in subject and so admirably executed by one of our native and most celebrated sculptors. We trust it may find a fitting place in the great Park which is so much admired and appreciated not only by our own citizens, but by all who visit the great metropolis."

Green responded, saying, in part, "The Commissioners of the Park, fully concurring in your high estimation of the ability shown by the eminent artist in the conception and execution of this beautiful work, will, with peculiar satisfaction, add its great attractions to those already existing in the Park."

Nearly a year and a half later the statue was unveiled on the Mall. The *Indian Hunter* sat high upon a white marble base. In describing the work, the *New York Times* said on April 23, 1869, "The figures are finely executed, and are better worthy of the attention than any group of statuary yet placed in the Park." It was the first statue placed in Central Park by an American artist.

By 1903 the neglected condition of the Central Park statues prompted a full-scale, nearly year-long cleaning by the Parks Department. F. Edwin Elwell, curator of the statuary department of the Metropolitan Museum of Art had suggested the project, and he personally directed it. The *Indian Hunter* had special needs.

"The Indian Hunter, the well known statue by J.Q.A. Ward in Central Park, just west of the Mall, was a favorite hiding place for large colonies of the municipality's wasps," said the *Sun* on September 18, 1903. "The mud tenements of these strenuous little insects were plastered thickly over the surface both of the hunter and the dog in the group. In the corner of one of the eyes of the man, and also in one of the dog's eyes, there were wasps' nests, giving the man a decided squint and the dog a very droll appearance."

By now the statue had received a replacement base of polished granite, possibly made necessary by the erosion of the original marble. Four colors of stone create the pedestal: the topmost section was updated around the turn of the century with carved cross-hatching.

The Indian Hunter received a replacement bronze bow in 1937 after the original was vandalized, and in 1992 the sculpture was fully restored. Among the oldest statues in the park, it marks a turning point in American art and in the career of the artist who conceived it.

CENTRAL PARK CAROUSEL

CENTRAL PARK

Included in the original designs for Central Park was a children's area where Victorian youngsters could play in the fresh, open air and enjoy amusements not available elsewhere in the city. Among those amusements was a carousel.

At the time the term referred variously to the ride or the building that housed it. In his 1882 *New York by Sunlight and Gaslight*, James D. McCabe, Jr., wrote "A few steps north of the swings is 'The Carrousel,' a circular building, fitted up with hobby horses and merry go rounds, for the amusement of younger children."

The "hobby horses and merry go rounds" (there was actually only one) McCabe described were gaily colored and fantastic—certain to captivate young imaginations. Opened in 1871, the great turntable ran on mule power. As children laughed in delight, riding their wooden painted steeds above, a mule in a pit below ground powered the mechanism along. The animals, plodding along on a treadmill, were trained to stop and go when the operator stomped his boot on the carousel floor.

In May of 1886 Park Commissioners proposed an edict against amusements in the Park on Sundays—a motion that elicited rapid response from the public. Commissioner John D. Crimmins admitted that, "The carousel was the special delight of small boys. No complaints had been made against these amusements."

The public opinion won out and the carousel kept turning.

The city was captivated in the spring of 1905 as the *New York Times* readers followed the story of 5-year-old tourist Marie Van Mater of Denver who, while riding the carousel, had carefully laid her rag doll, Herbert, on the ground nearby. The little girl had done so because the lion on which she rode "was so fierce that she feared for Herbert."

After the girl had ridden several times, she found Herbert had been stolen. She was so distraught that the staff of the Netherland Hotel where her family was staying scoured the Park around the carousel and her mother posted an ad in the *Times*:

"LOST—At merry-go-round or carrousel in Central Park, on Sunday, April 16, one rag doll; $5 reward for return to Netherland, 5th Av. And 59th."

The gaily-painted figures date from the turn of the last century.

The hotel was besieged with people carrying dolls, claiming to have found them in the Park. "Five dollars reward tempted those who were foolish enough to imagine that a five-year old girl would not know her own precious Herbert from every other doll on earth," said the *New York Times.*

In the end a little impoverished waif returned Herbert, refusing the reward because she had stolen him. Another story from the carousel ended happily.

In 1912 the days of underground mule power were, happily for the mules, a thing of the past when an electric motor was installed. Then in 1924 the carousel burned to the ground.

A new carousel spun merrily along until November of 1950 when this one, too, burned. "The Central Park carousel, dear to the hearts of small New Yorkers since 1871, was ruined by fire before dawn yesterday. Its forty-four gaudy wooden steeds were charred into black immobility, while fire and water combined to halt its mechanism and silence its carnival music," reported the *Times.*

A search for a suitable replacement was initiated. Amazingly, a wonderful, if derelict, carousel carved by the Brooklyn firm of Stein & Goldstein between 1908 and 1911 was found abandoned in an old trolley terminal at Coney Island. Upon receiving a $107,000 gift on July 2, 1951 from the Michael Friedsam Foundation that included a new building, the New York City Parks Department restored the ride

The life-like horses were carved between 1908 and 1911.

at its Randall's Island facility, repainting the nearly life-sized horses and updating the equipment before the return to Central Park.

On July 3, 1951, the carousel was spinning again with free rides on that opening day. Mayor Impellitteri rode a chestnut charger along with other politicians and hordes of shouting children.

With fifty-seven hand-carved horses and two chariots, the carousel is one of the largest in the country and considered one of the finest examples of American turn-of-the-century folk art in existence. The vintage Ruth & Sohn band organ was modified to play Wurlitzer Style 150 paper music rolls by Carousel Works of Mansfield, Ohio.

In the 1990s the Central Park Conservancy funded new landscaping around the carousel and, once again, the restoration of the horses. More recently, the band organ was refurbished by Gavin McDonough.

Throughout the years, the carousel has attracted young and old, rich and not-so-rich ("Mrs. John F. Kennedy rode the horses on the Central Park carousel shortly before noon yesterday with her son, John Jr." reported *The Times* in 1964).

Today the ride costs $3.00, up from fifty cents in 1871, providing entertainment to nearly 250,000 riders every year.

Rag dolls ride for free.

UPPER EAST SIDE

ROOSEVELT HOUSES,
47-49 EAST 65TH STREET

169 EAST 71ST STREET

123 EAST 73RD STREET

ROOSEVELT HOUSES

47–49 EAST 65TH STREET

Sara Ann Delano, who could trace her ancestors to the *Mayflower*, married the wealthy widower James Roosevelt in 1880. They had one son, Franklin. After James Roosevelt's death in 1900, the domineering Sara doted even more on her already cosseted son.

Two years later, Franklin, by then a Harvard student, met his distant cousin, Anna Eleanor Roosevelt. Following a reception and dinner on New Year's Eve, 1902, at the White House (President Theodore Roosevelt was Eleanor's uncle), the two began seeing one another. Within a year, in November, Franklin proposed.

Sara Delano Roosevelt was not pleased.

On her insistence, the engagement was not announced for a month while she argued against the marriage. Then, in 1904, Sara swept her son away on a cruise in the hopes that separation would bring him to his senses. It didn't.

"I know what pain I must have caused you," Franklin wrote to his mother, referring to the engagement, "I know my mind, have known it for a long time, and know that I could never think otherwise."

Much to Sara's disappointment, Franklin and Eleanor were married on St. Patrick's Day, 1905, with President Roosevelt giving away the bride.

The newlyweds took an apartment and then left for a three-month honeymoon. They returned to find that Sara Roosevelt had started plans for a double townhouse for the three of them—Franklin and his new wife on one side, she on the other.

Designed by architect Charles A. Platt, the house was completed in 1908. Situated on East 65th Street near Fifth Avenue, it was a stately red-brick neo-Georgian structure on a limestone base. The arched doorway with double wrought-iron doors framed a handsome fanlight. The foyer beyond contained the doors leading to the separate residences.

At the second floor, with its four tall, multi-paned windows, a wrought-iron balcony extended the width of the structure. A striking carved cartouche between the third and fourth stories added visual interest.

Sara took up residence in No. 47, while Franklin and Eleanor moved in next door

Sara poses with Franklin in a highlands outfit in 1887.

at No. 49. Totally dominating the couple's lives, Sara chose their furniture and décor and hired their household staff.

The couple stayed in the house when they were in New York, which, as the years passed, became less and less.

In 1918 the Spanish flu pandemic swept the globe. More than a quarter of the world's population was infected and between 50 and 100 million died. On September 17 of that year, Franklin Roosevelt, now Assistant Secretary of the Navy, arrived in New York after two months abroad. Roosevelt had contracted the dreaded disease aboard ship, and it had now worsened with pneumonia. Rather than being taken to his own home, where Eleanor was waiting, he was taken to his mother's side of the residence.

Three years later, in August of 1921, Franklin was abruptly stricken with polio. After two months of hospitalization, he insisted on going to East 65th Street, rather than to the more private Hyde Park estate upstate. Here, in the fourth-floor bedroom, he spent months in a resolute struggle to recover and resume his political and social life.

However, gradually Franklin and Eleanor spent less time at No. 49 until, by 1928, the family was there only sporadically. After her husband's election to the White

The two homes were designed to appear as a single refined mansion.

House, Eleanor preferred to spend her time she had in New York at an apartment at 20 East 11th Street in Greenwich Village. Finally, in October, 1934, the *New York Times* reported that "President Roosevelt's town house at 47–49 East Sixty-fifth Street is for rent. A rectangular sign saying so, freshly coated with cream-colored paint and lettered in bright ultramarine, was hung to the right of the arched doorway yesterday morning."

Mrs. James Roosevelt, however, remained firmly entrenched. Sara gave regular teas in support of her many charities, and the door to her side of the residence welcomed a steady stream of New York socialites until 1941.

Perhaps the first hint that things were not well with Sara was when, on September 5 of that year, Eleanor gave up her 11th Street apartment and moved back into the home on 65th Street (which the *New York Times* noted "has stood unoccupied for most of the period since her husband went to the White House in 1933"). Eleanor told the press her move was in part economical but that she "will be next door to the President's mother, who has not been in good health."

Two days later, Sara Delano Roosevelt was dead.

After a week had passed, Eleanor Roosevelt instructed the real estate firm of Pease & Elliman to put the house on the market. In October, the President and Eleanor went through the house for the last time to select "furniture and bric-a-brac that he wants to transfer to his home at Hyde Park on the Hudson," reported the *Times*.

The property was acquired in 1942 by a group who presented it to Hunter College as a social and interfaith center. Franklin Roosevelt expressed his happiness regarding the home's new use, which was to foster "mutual understanding among Protestant, Jewish and Catholic students." The joined houses, he said, brought "memories of joy and sorrow."

Eleanor Roosevelt spoke at the dedication ceremonies.

The President personally furnished the library and presented a large number of books. The two dining rooms were combined as were the two parlors; but otherwise the interiors were kept essentially intact.

Today, the dignified double home that Sara Delano Roosevelt built looks just as it did in 1908. It is a fine example of early twentieth-century townhouse architecture and an important piece of American history.

WILLIAMSBURG ON THE UPPER EAST SIDE

123 EAST 73RD STREET

The first years of the twentieth century saw a renewed interest in things Colonial, an interest that was reflected in domestic architecture. Suddenly, interspersed among the marble and limestone chateaux and palazzos of New York's wealthy were brick-and-stone Neo-Federal and Neo-Georgian structures such as Andrew Carnegie's 1903 mansion on upper Fifth Avenue.

In November 1902, William M. Benjamin purchased three brownstone houses at Nos. 119, 121, and 123 East 73rd Street. The neighborhood was quickly changing into a highly fashionable one and within days he had resold the plots. The old townhouses would not survive much longer. No. 123 went to "a buyer who will erect thereon a high-class dwelling," reported the *New York Times*.

The buyer was architect Robert Burnside Potter, a member of the firm Robertson & Potter. He designed and erected a neo-Georgian brick-and-limestone mansion, construction of which began in 1903 and was completed a year later. By secreting the fourth floor behind a wooden railing, set back in the mansard roof, the architects gave the appearance and proportions of a smaller building.

The title to the completed house was put in the name of Robert Potter's wife, Elizabeth. But it would soon become home to Dr. Frederic Grosvenor Goodridge who had married Ethel Iselin two years earlier. Goodridge came from a socially prominent family and his new wife was descended from three Colonial-period families—Morris, Gouveneur and Philipse. The eighteenth century-inspired home was therefore especially appropriate for the couple.

Colonial detailing—splayed keystones above the first- and second-story windows, a carved shell within the pediment over the doorway, a recessed and paneled entrance, and a wonderful scrolled, broken pediment on the middle dormer—lent authenticity to the design. An American basement was protected by a restrained wooden fence.

Mrs. Goodridge established herself quickly as an accomplished hostess. Elaborate entertainments were held here for the cream of society. On January 28, 1910, the house was the scene of a dinner dance. Sixty guests were invited for

The Goodridge mansion was among the finest of New York City's Colonial-inspired structures.

dinner at 8:00 p.m., after which an additional hundred arrived for dancing and a midnight buffet supper.

The splendid home at 123 East 73rd Street proved, eventually, inadequate for Ethel Goodridge's entertaining, and later in 1910 they purchased two brownstone houses on East 78th Street, where they constructed a double-width mansion, also in the Neo-Georgian style.

The 73rd Street house came to the Carlfen family. But shortly after their move to East 73rd Street, the family was hit by tragedy, when on the afternoon of June 19 1910, West 73rd 20-year-old Robert Carlfen drowned while swimming at Coney Island.

Within four years the house was owned by George W. Miller, whose new 1914 Pierce Arrow motorcar would have been admired on the street. The elderly man's household was filled with extended family. Both daughters (who had coincidentally married men named Peabody) and their families were in the house. Mary Chester Miller Peabody's husband, Richard, had died.

1914 opened with debutante entertainments for Mary's daughter Constance Peabody. And it ended with a tea, dinner, and dancing for Priscilla Peabody (daughter of Mr. and Mrs. Stephen Peabody) for her debut.

Two years later, on April 26, 1916, Mary Chester Miller Peabody married the 49-year-old Augustus Rene Moen. Moen listed himself as a real estate broker; however, his myriad positions included Director and Treasurer of the Rutland & Whiting Co., Director and Vice-President of the Fowler Mfg. Co., and Director and Treasurer of the Panstock Co. Within two years the newlyweds had two more children, Edward and Mary. Everyone was still living in the East 73rd Street house.

But by the early 1920s the Millers, Peabodys, and Moens had moved on and the house was owned by attorney Frank Longfellow Crocker, the senior member of Crocker, Johnson & Shores at 5 Nassau Street. The family owned a country estate in North Haven, Maine. When daughter Elizabeth returned from school in Paris in 1922, her engagement to a Cleveland businessman was announced.

On November 5 the *Times* reported that Elizabeth's wedding to Henry Gilbert Hold "took place quietly yesterday noon at the residence of the bride's parents, 123 East Seventy-third Street, the Rev. Dr. Henry Evertson Cobb officiating in the presence of the families and a few close friends." It was a low-key function compared to the entertaining the house had experienced under Ethel Goodridge.

On January 16, 1931, an "international marriage of more than usual interest took place," as *The Times* put it. Barbara Schieffelin had a social pedigree nearly unmatched in New York. The great-great-great-granddaughter of John Jay, first Chief Justice of the United States, and a direct descendant of Commodore Cornelius Vanderbilt, she married Charles Ion Carr Bosanquet of Northumberland, England.

The Madison Avenue Presbyterian Church was filled with the most notable names of New York society for the wedding. Among them were the bride's sister, Margaret Louise Schieffelin Osborn and her husband, Frederick H. Osborn, the most recent owners of 123 East 73rd Street.

Following the ceremony, the Osborns hosted a reception. The house "was decorated with rosary ferns, white carnations and forsythia," commented the *Times*.

Osborn also came from a distinguished family, dating to the seventeenth century in America, and was the grandson of millionaire William Earl Dodge. Osborn's family had made a fortune in the railroad business. During World War I he served in the American Red Cross in France as Commander of the Advance Zone. By the time he purchased No. 123 East 73rd Street, he was a research associate at the American Museum of Natural History, studying anthropology and population. It was a course of life that would have resounding ramifications later.

The Osborns, who divided their time between 73rd Street and their Garrison, New York, estate, were highly involved in progressive reforms. Osborn was one of the founding members of the American Eugenics Society and was fundamental in the creation of Princeton University's Office of Population Research. He is credited with advancements in the understanding that environment plays a greater role than race in IQ levels.

In the meantime, Mrs. Osborn was making her own mark. In 1937, the year that daughter Margery's engagement was announced, she held a series of discussions in the home on "Education for Democracy."

With the onset of World War II, Franklin Roosevelt selected Osborn to chair the Civilian Advisory Committee on Selective Service in 1940. Before the year was ended, he took over as Chair of the Army Committee on Welfare and Recreation and the Osborns left East 73rd Street for Washington, D.C. By the end of the war, now a Major General, Frederick Osborn had earned the Distinguished Service Medal, the Selective Service Medal, a bronze star, and he was made Honorary Commander of the Order of the British Empire.

At mid-century the house was owned by Osborn's daughter, Mrs. Margery O. Erickson, who converted it to two residences—a lower triplex and a separate duplex on the top two floors. She sold it in 1952 to Evelyn W. Backer. Backer held the property only for a year, selling it in August 1953 to Michel Pierre Fribourg and his wife. The couple announced plans to live in the lower triplex after they returned from a scheduled European trip.

Fribourg was a Belgium-born American who came to New York at the outbreak of World War II to work in his family's business (he had been headquartered in the London office previously). He became a citizen, served in the U.S. Army, and took over the business, Conti-Group Companies, after his father's death.

In 1964, Fribourg attained an unexpected notoriety. That year he announced the sale of $80 million of wheat and rice to the Soviet Union. Fribourg was humble. "Anybody can get grain to sell to the Soviet Union," he said. "Our business is basically built on ideas and imagination."

The real significance of the deal, he felt, was that it proved that trade could create communication that simple diplomacy could not.

Fribourg was founding director of the U.S.-U.S.S.R. Trade and Economic Council and the U.S.-China Business Council. His charitable works included the Fribourg Foundation and the Conti-Group Foundation, and he contributed generously to schools and hospitals.

Michel Fribourg died in April 2001 at the age of 87. The new buyers of No. 123 East 73rd Street reconverted the house to a single-family residence.

Today, the remarkable Neo-Georgian house with its equally remarkable history sits like a small sliver of Williamsburg, Virginia, on a stylish side street of the Upper East Side, quite unchanged since its completion in 1904.

SOCIAL TRAGEDY AND CINEMATIC HISTORY

169 EAST 71ST STREET

Much has been made of the exterior of the row house at 169 East 71ˢᵗ Street as the "Breakfast at Tiffany's" home of Holly Golightly. When the Victorian house came on the market in December 2011 for $5.85 million, it garnered renewed attention. New Yorkers have forgotten, however, that the house made famous in the 1961 motion picture had previously played an important role in an unnerving footnote of Manhattan history.

In the second half of the nineteenth century, the Upper East Side filled with comfortable homes built for upper- and upper-middle-class families. Developers built blocks of near carbon-copy homes, many in the extremely popular Anglo-Italianate style.

Joseph Wallace Cremin purchased one such house in 1876, at 169 East 71ˢᵗ Street. Cremin was an educator who began his career prior to 1844 teaching in the western part of New York State. In 1858 he came to New York City, teaching in Grammar School No. 1. Afterwards he moved on to Grammar School No. 18 and, when the new Grammar School No. 27 was opened, he was made principal.

Cremin and his wife reared their sizable family in the house. Life in the Cremin home was mostly uneventful; however, it certainy became exciting when, on August 25, 1883, John E. Moore, along with Mart Allen and Michael Thomas, broke into and burgled the house. The thieves later received sentences of between five and ten years in the state prison.

In 1895, at the age of 73, Joseph Cremin submitted his request to the Trustees of the Nineteenth Ward asking to be granted retirement. The school principal cited his "declining years and length of service" as reasons to be allowed to retire. The Trustees honored his request, noting that "There are few younger men than Dr. Cremin for his years, but he has earned his honors and now desires to give way for younger men."

Seven years later, on August 4, 1902, the 80-year-old Joseph Cremin died in the family home at 169 East 71ˢᵗ Street.

The year following his father's death, Stephen E. Cremin's wife left him, and he moved back into the 71ˢᵗ Street house where his brothers and sisters still lived.

Stephen was a traveling salesman whose territory was in the South.

Stephen's 18-year-old son, Victor Thomas (who for some reason went by the name of William), lived away at a military boarding school, and Adeline, his 14-year-old daughter, lived with her mother in Larchmont, New York. Stephen Cremin had many friends and was a member of the Larchmont Yacht Club, the New York Athletic Club, the Lambs Club, and, according to Dr. O. M. Leiser, who had known Cremin for years, "of practically all the leading clubs and social organizations in the South."

Yet the separation deeply affected him. He was subject to periods of deep depression that were noticed by his friends and fellow club members. On February 11, 1915, Cremin walked into the Lambs Club around 5:00 p.m. seemingly in good spirits, and chatted with several members.

After a while he requested a room, saying he wanted to rest. Bellboys, around eight in the evening, heard groans coming from the room and called for help.

Cremin was found lying across the bed when the door was forced open. He had taken a razor to his throat and

Although a bit careworn, the Victorian rowhouse retains its original architectural elements.

to his wrists. Despite a doctor's attempts to save him, he died at 9:30 from loss of blood. A letter left on the bureau read in part, "I am tired and have decided to go. I prefer to be cremated. After the ashes are swept up 'tis my desire that they be thrown to the winds from the roof of the Lambs Club."

Regarding his funeral, he requested that Father Lavelle and Dr. Houghton of the Little Church Around the Corner officiate. With a posthumous sense of humor, he said, "I would like my dear friend Wilton Lackaye, if he wishes, to say a few words. He tells the truth, but I hope he won't tell it about me."

Cremin asked that his sister, Nell, take care of his daughter and that his friend George Loft see to having his son appointed to West Point. He ended his suicide letter, "Forgive me, fellow Lambs."

The emotional and moving letter was published in several newspapers, and New Yorkers remembered the incident for years.

One of Stephen's brothers, Joseph Daniel Cremin, who was Deputy Tax Commissioner under the Tammany administration, died in the house four years later in July 1919.

The extensive Cremin family was gone from No. 169 East 71st Street by 1947 when it was converted to a two-family home—one duplex apartment in the basement and parlor floor, another taking up the second and third floors. The handsome building has remained a two-family house since then—not quite the multi-apartment configuration in which Holly Golightly sang "Moon River."

The house was purchased in 2000 for $1.88 million by Peter E. Bacanovic, the then-Merrill Lynch broker who later found himself in hot water over the Martha Stewart insider-trading case in 2002. Some interior renovations were executed by architect David Gauld; then, in December 2011, Bacanovic put the Victorian townhouse on the market again for $6 million. It became available again in 2014 for $10 million.

While the prim row house will perhaps always be remembered as the home of Truman Capote's Holly Golightly, Edwardian New Yorkers thought of it for many years as the home of Stephen Cremin—the house which the emotionally devastated salesman left for his last drink at the Lambs Club.

HARLEM

17 EAST 128TH STREET

HARRIET TUBMAN STATUE
WEST 122ND STREET
ST. NICHOLAS AVENUE AND
FREDERICK DOUGLASS BOULEVARD

DYCKMAN FARMHOUSE,
BROADWAY AND 204TH STREET

A REMARKABLE SURVIVOR

17 EAST 128TH STREET

In 1658 Peter Stuyvesant, the last Dutch Director-General of the colony of New Netherland, visited the countryside at the northern end of Manhattan island and named it after the Dutch city of Haarlem.

More than a day's travel from the city, the Harlem area developed into a mixture of Dutch farms with humble homesteads and the country estates of New York's wealthy—the Beekmans, Hamiltons, Gracies, and Rikers among them. The rural nature of Harlem continued until the first years of the Civil War.

In 1837 the Harlem Railroad extended as far north as 129th Street and in 1856 steamboat service was available in the summer. Real estate developers recognized the significant potential of Harlem as a New York City suburb and gradually began residential development in the 1860s. East 128th Street was among the first to see row houses crop up and in 1864 the block between Fifth and Madison Avenues was lined with attractive frame houses in the latest French Second Empire style.

The architectural style had become all the rage during the Paris Exhibition of 1852. It spread first to England, then to America—and the houses on East 128th Street were at the cutting edge of architectural fashion. Among them was No. 17, a two-story home with the obligatory mansard roof. The parlor floor was perched above a high, red brick English basement and fronted by a wide, commodious front porch.

The handsome double doors were framed by a sculptured arched entranceway and topped by a half-round overlight. Floor-to-ceiling windows allowed sunlight to flood the parlor and circulated air in the stifling summers. The roof of the porch, supported by wooden ornamental scrollwork brackets, wore a fringe of lacy gingerbread carpentry.

Above it all, three handsome pronounced dormers pierced the multicolored slate tiles of the mansard roof. The house was set back from the sidewalk to provide a small garden behind the wooden fence that matched the porch railing.

In 1865 Samuel M. Brown sold No. 17 to James Beach, who was living in Throgs Neck in Westchester County, New York. Beach paid $5,900 for the property—nearly $150,000 today.

The sleepy community was shaken awake by the arrival of the elevated railroads at the end of the 1870s. With the neighborhood now more accessible, an explosion of development occurred. In 1874 Beach sold the house to Jacob Van Reed and his wife, Hannah, for $11,000. The Van Reeds owned the house a dozen years before moving on.

East 128th Street was home, for the most part, to professionals, and in 1886 attorney Hubert A. Banning purchased No. 17, putting the deed in his wife's name as was common practice in the nineteenth and early twentieth centuries. Banning paid $12,000 for the house. Thirty years later, on Thursday, January 6, 1916, his funeral was held in the parlor here.

Viola Banning continued to reside in the house, along with her son Hubert, also a lawyer,

The charming wooden residence is like a Victorian dollhouse.

and his wife, Anna Olga. Hubert Banning was an active member of the American Oriental Society.

As World War I drew to a close, the block along East 128th Street remained home to white-collar residents. Next door at No. 15 was the elderly retired pharmacist George W. Busteed, who invented "The Sun Cholera Cure" during the cholera epidemic of 1849. Down the block was Dr. James F. Campbell at No. 43, while schoolteacher Mary A. Martin was living at No. 56.

But by now No. 17 was one of the last of the 1860s houses left. Most had been demolished to be replaced by late nineteenth-century brownstone row houses or apartment buildings.

By the mid 1920s, Hubert and Anna Banning were living in Germany. His mother, Viola, who was at this time the President of the Gillette Clipping Machine Company (later to become the Gillette Company, best known for its razor blades and shavers)

By 1930, No. 17 was vised in between two larger structures. The wooden fence, while missing a post or two, still remained.

remained on in the house. In his absence, Hubert named Palmer A. Brooks as trustee, giving him authority to sell the property should anything happen to Viola.

Shortly thereafter, on June 15, 1926, Viola Suydam Banning died. Brooks sold the charming Victorian house to Margaret Lane for $12,000, the exact amount Banning's father had paid forty years earlier. Margaret Lane remained in the house only seven years before transferring the property to siblings Louis and May Seeley for the astonishing amount of $1.00. The mystery of the $1 sale was explained in 1979 when the 90-year-old Louis Seeley sold the property. He explained to the buyer that Margaret Lane had been Louis's and May's nanny.

In the nearly half-century that Louis Seeley lived in the house at No. 17, both Harlem and East 128th Street had changed. A large school now stood across the street and the wood frame house was squeezed between two much larger late Victorian structures. Yet, amazingly, the little house was intact. The original fence was gone, but the beautiful Victorian doors, the slate roof, and the ornamental wooden detailing of the front porch were all still there.

The house was purchased by the Director of the Harlem Dance Studio, Carolyn Adams, who fortunately was interested in historic preservation and the fostering of community pride within the Harlem neighborhood. The dollhouse-like home at 17 East 128th Street sold again in 2011 for just under $1.8 million.

This remarkable survivor is one of the few remaining frame houses in Harlem dating to the Civil War period. That it remained a single-family home for over a century and a half, in nearly pristine condition, is just short of a miracle.

SWING LOW—
THE HARRIET TUBMAN STATUE
WEST 122ND STREET AT ST. NICHOLAS AVENUE
AND FREDERICK DOUGLASS BOULEVARD

Araminta "Minty" Ross was born into slavery around 1822 in Dorchester County, Maryland. Determined and unwilling to submit to forced servitude, she escaped to Philadelphia in 1849 with the help of the already-established Underground Railroad.

Having attained her personal freedom and safety, Ross turned her attention to those she left behind. The Underground Railroad had already helped an estimated 100,000 slaves in their escape; now one of them would be a major force in assisting many more. To help disguise her identity, Ross changed her name to Harriet Tubman.

Throughout the next decade, the resolute woman traveled back and forth into slave territory to help slaves escape along the Underground Railroad to their freedom in the North. When the Civil War erupted, she offered her services as a nurse to the Union Army, then doubled her usefulness by working as a spy. Her greatest triumph came on June 1, 1863, when she guided the Union Army to the Combahee Ferry in South Carolina.

A year earlier, Tubman had been assigned by the Army to Beaufort, South Carolina, to nurse former slaves on the Sea Islands. As Union commanders planned coastal river raids, including on the Combahee, she was called upon to supply intelligence. On the evening of June 1, Harriet Tubman was aboard the *John Adams*, one of three U.S. Navy ships carrying 300 soldiers—all former slaves.

As the Union ships passed the plantation fields along shore, hundreds of slaves dropped their farm tools and crowded the riverbank, pleading to be taken aboard. The two-day operation was not only a military success, but resulted in the freeing of over 750 slaves.

The uneducated Harriet Tubman was called upon to make her first public address. Union Brigadier General Rufus Saxton praised her, calling her the only woman to plan and lead a military raid. Apparently unaware of Tubman's name, the *Commonwealth* reported "Colonel Montgomery and his gallant band of 300 black soldiers under the guidance of a black woman, dashed into the enemy's country,

Harriet Tubman posed for a cabinet card photograph by H. B. Lindsley in the years after the Civil War.

struck a bold and effective blow, destroying millions of dollars worth of commissary stores, cotton and lordly dwellings, and striking terror into the heart of rebeldom, brought off nearly 800 slaves and thousands of dollars worth of property, without losing a man or receiving a scratch. It was a glorious consummation…. The Colonel was followed by a speech from the black woman who led the raid and under whose inspiration it was originated and conducted. For sound sense and real native eloquence her address would do honor to any man, and it created a great sensation."

The cause of black Americans did not die for Harriet Tubman with the end of the Civil War. She continued to work not only for racial equality, but for women's rights. She toiled tirelessly for Woman's Suffrage, working closely with Susan B. Anthony, and later became an activist for the homeless and physically disabled.

In 1911, Harriet Tubman was "ill and penniless," according to a New York newspaper. The elderly woman, once such a powerful force in human rights, was now frail and helpless. She was admitted into a rest home that had been named in her honor. She died there of pneumonia in 1913.

Nearly a century later, in 2007, the City of New York's Department of Cultural Affairs Percent for Art Program sponsored a sculptural memorial to Tubman. The program was initiated by Mayor Edward Koch in 1982. The law requires that one percent of the budget for City-funded construction is spent on artwork for City facilities. Artist Alison Saar was given the commission to design the statue. A 1978 alumna of Scripps College, she had studied African and Caribbean Art there.

Saar's powerful two-ton statue of Tubman named *Swing Low* was placed in Harlem in a triangular traffic island at West 122nd Street, St. Nicholas Avenue, and Frederick Douglass Boulevard. Dedicated on November 13, 2008, it emanates determination and fortitude.

Reflecting her work in the Underground Railroad, Tubman's body pushes forward like a locomotive, her arms churning at her side like the pistons of train wheels. Her skirt is slightly pulled up at the front, showing her petticoats like the cow-catcher of a steam locomotive. Tubman's face stares straight forward in resolve to attain her goal.

Symbols of freedom from slavery—broken chains, a key, a padlock, for instance—cover the skirt. The uprooting of tyranny and inequality is represented in the trail of roots Tubman drags behind her.

Saar covered Tubman's skirt with the faces of freed slaves. Interspersed are common articles—an iron key representing their slavery, worn shoe soles, a padlock, shackles with a broken chain. A trail of roots stretch from the back of Tubman's skirt: a tradition of oppression uprooted and powerless thanks partly to the indefatigable efforts of one determined former slave who would not forget those she left behind.

Immediately following the dedication of the statue came controversy concerning its orientation. Harriet Tubman is striding resolutely southward. Local residents complained that she should be heading northward—away from the tyranny of the South. A petition of 1,000 signatures was sent to the City, calling for the statue to be turned around.

Jacob Morris, director of the Harlem Historical Society, said, "It is just an outrage."

The sculptor disagreed. Alison Saar explained to Timothy Williams of the *New York Times*: "She's best known for her sojourns north, but what is most impressive to me are her trips south, where she risked her own freedom."

Authors, historians, artists, and residents still debate the statue's geographic orientation today. But Saar's commanding memorial to an exceptional woman stands unquestioned.

DYCKMAN FARMHOUSE
BROADWAY AND 204TH STREET

When the American Revolution erupted in 1776, the Dyckman family had been farming upper Manhattan for nearly a century. Jan Dyckman, a German immigrant from Westphalia, arrived in the Dutch settlement below what is now Wall Street and soon thereafter purchased several hundred acres far to the north where he established his farm in 1661.

As land was added, the Dyckman farm stretched from river to river and roughly from today's 213th Street south to the 190s. The original Dyckman farmhouse was located near the Spuyten Duyvil Creek, at Manhattan's northernmost point.

As time passed, wealthy country squires established estates in the area. The Dyckmans, however, referred to their land as a farm and famously raised cabbages and cherries. A second, larger house nearer to the Harlem River replaced the original.

The Revolution would change the idyllic atmosphere of the farm.

Jan's grandson, William, had inherited the land. Known Loyalists, the Dyckmans fled north to Westchester in 1776 when British General Howe moved northward after the Battle of Long Island and took the Apthorpe Mansion in Bloomingdale, just to the south of the farm, in anticipation of the coming Battle of Harlem. After that conflict, the Continental Army took possession of the Dyckman house for a short time, followed by the British, who occupied it until 1783.

The Dyckman family returned that year to find that the British had burned their home and their orchards to the ground. Undeterred, William's eldest son, Jacobus, with the help of slaves, rebuilt it between 1783 and 1785. Set on a stony bluff, the house was built of fieldstone, brick, and wood, with the upper story of clapboard. Characteristic of the Dutch Colonial style so familiar to the family was the high basement and the low-pitched gambrel roof, curved to swing over a full-length porch. Two large parlors and two private bedrooms comprised the main floor, the second story being a large open loft space. A winter kitchen doubled as a heating source, while a separate summer kitchen in the garden, with a small bedroom area above for, most likely, a cook, was used in hotter months.

The farmhouse as it appeared around 1934.

The orchards on the 250-acre farm were replanted, and in 1787 when William died, the farm had a barn, a cider mill, and several outbuildings. Jacobus took over the farm, moving his sizable family (eventually totaling eleven children) into the homestead.

As time passed, Jacobus—who became New York City Alderman in 1822—renovated the home, partitioning off bedrooms upstairs in the 1820s and adding a wing to the north around 1830. In 1820 the building housed ten people including Jacobus (whose wife had died in 1814), three sons, a grandson, a niece, a white woman and a freed black woman, one male slave and one freed black boy. Other family members and workers lived in three other homes spotted around the farm.

After Jacobus died in 1832, his sons Michael and Isaac lived on in the home for another two decades. Michael died in 1854 and Isaac erected a more modern home near Spuyten Duyvil, where he died in 1868.

Upon his death 128 acres of land, divided into 151 plots, were auctioned off. "This is the largest quantity of land ever offered for sale at one time within the City limits," said the *New York Times*. Two years later, another 92 acres, divided into 900 lots, were auctioned. The subsequent lay-out of new streets would place the Dyckman homestead at the corner of Broadway and 204th Street.

In the later years of the nineteenth century, socially prominent John H. Judge and his wife, Winifred, purchased the house at auction. Although the *New York Times* remarked, "It fell into good hands, for Mr. Judge has guarded the old place from damage as jealously as if it were the home of his ancestors," period photographs show the building in a state of serious neglect.

The Judges never lived in the home, residing instead in their mansion at 27 West 94th Street. In November 1913 the couple announced their intention to give the house to the Daughters of the Revolution to convert it into a museum. The caveat was that the Judges wanted to keep the valuable land on which the home stood— "Mr. Judge, however, has stipulated that the building must be placed on a satisfactory site in Isham Park," noted the *Times*.

Despite the city's promises, appropriations for the new site and moving costs were not forthcoming. In May 1914 the Art Commission photographed the Dyckman House, along with other threatened historic buildings, as part of an architectural record. The future of the colonial building was shaky at best.

In an eerie coincidence, on December 18, 1914, Winifred Judge and Fannie Dyckman, widow of Isaac Dyckman, both died. Spurred by the death of their mother, Mary Alice Dyckman Dean and Fannie Fredericka Dyckman Welch purchased their family home to rescue it and present it to the city as a memorial to their parents.

As luck would have it, Mary's husband was Bashford Dean of the Metropolitan Museum of Art and Columbia University, and Fannie's husband was architect Alexander M. Welch. While the sisters gathered family furniture and relics for the museum, their husbands spent over a year restoring the structure. Welch oversaw the restoration while Dean worked on the interiors. The architect carefully removed features not original to the house, such as the 1830s addition. By July 1916, it was ready for presentation to the city.

"It is doubtful if any old house in the country has ever been restored with such care to preserve its former features," reported the *Times*. "To get hand-hewn timbers and other old material with which to make necessary repairs, Mr. Welch purchased two century-old houses about to be torn down in New Jersey and part of many others. Every lock and bolt is more than eighty years old, and scores of hand-made nails were used. In the house itself little actual restoration was required, but the old smokehouse in the rear has been restored, as originally built."

On the ground floor, a room was set apart to display Revolutionary and Native American relics excavated on the Dyckman property and a Hessian hut was rebuilt behind the house, using original bricks. A year later the sisters purchased two additional lots adjoining the house as a gift to the city. "The additional property will make it possible to enlarge the garden, which had been laid out in old Dutch style," said *The Times*.

While a laudable early example of architectural preservation, the restored rooms more closely reflected the Edwardian romanticized view of colonial life than the more realistic hardships endured by eighteenth-century farmers. Helen W. Henderson in her 1917 *A Loiterer in New York* was not impressed, calling it an "almost too clean restoration."

"Its proportions are unpretentious, for it was a simple farmhouse," continued Henderson, "but the two Dyckman daughters, who presented it to the city, in

Sitting within a swath of green amid an urban landscape, the eighteenth century farmhouse miraculously survives.

1916, have spared no trouble or expense in outfitting it with family heirlooms and Revolutionary trophies found in the neighbourhood, and in making the house as homelike and intimate as a public museum can hope to be."

Controversy swirled around the museum when in 1918, while the U.S. was embroiled in the First World War, German-born Park Commissioner William F. Grell abruptly dismissed the curator and another employee and replaced them with Captain Frederick Hensler and his wife "who are of German birth, but naturalized here," according to *The Times*.

The newspaper went on to list Commissioner Grell's memberships in German clubs and societies and lament the "precarious circumstances" of the fired employees.

Today, the Dyckman Farmhouse Museum is owned by the New York City Department of Parks & Recreation. A member of the Historic House Trust, it is a New York City Landmark and is included on the National Register of Historic Places. Nestled among the modern buildings of Upper Broadway, the charming eighteenth-century house is both a surprise and a delight.

INDEX Page numbers in **bold** refer to illustrations

ACKNOWLEDGMENTS

Photographs © Alice Lum, with exception of the following;

Page 10: The *Police Gazette* 1891

Page 18: Bundesarchiv, Bild 102-10720 / CC-BY-SA

Page 22: Courtesy the Canal Park Inn

Page 41: Illustrated Catalogue of the Auction Sale of paintings from the collection of Frank Buckeley Smith, 1920

Page 43: Courtesy NYC Department of Records / Municipal Archives

Page 46: Source unknown

Pages 49 through 53: Vintage postcards from the author's collection

Page 63: The New York World, March 26, 1911

Page 64: *Jewish Journal*

Page 75: The National Archives General Slocum Disaster

Page 76: *Harper's Magazine* June 24, 1904

Page 89: King's Handbook of New York City, 1895

Page 90: The Architectural Record 1903

Page 95: King's Handbook of New York City, 1892

Page 102: National Gallery of Art, Washington DC

Pages 108 and 109: Vintage postcards from the author's collection

Page 111: Harvard College Class of 1897 25th Anniversary Report

Page 115: *Architects' and Builders' Magazine*, 1909

Page 116: The *Evening World*, July 22, 1911

Pages 120 and 121: Vintage postcards from the author's collection

Page 123: Author's collection

Page 125: Milstein Division of United States History, Local History & Genealogy, The New York Public Library

Page 136: The *New-York Tribune*, October 7, 1900

Page 147: Photo by Percy Loomis Sperr/copyright Milstein Division, The New York Public Library

Page 152: Photo by Gryffindor

Page 154: Courtesy Library of Congress Prints and Photographs Division, Washington DC

Page 168: Vintage postcard from the author's collection

Page 172: Vintage postcard from the author's collection

Page 176: Author's collection

Page 187: Courtesy Library of Congress Prints and Photographs Division, Washington DC

Page 192: "East 52nd Street at corner of 5th Avenue / Plant House"—by Wurts Bros. from the collection of the Museum of the City of New York

Page 195: Vintage postcard from the author's collection

Page 196: Sketch from *Town & Country* magazine, October 26, 1912

Page 198: Photo by Jim Henderson

Page 199: *Harper's Weekly,* October 26, 1864

Page 200: Courtesy Library of Congress Prints and Photographs Division, Washington DC

Page 213: Picture Collection, The New York Public Library, Astor, Lenox and Tilden Foundations

Page 212: Manual of the Corporation of the City of New York, 1869

Page 229: Franklin D. Roosevelt Library Public Domain Photographs

Page 242: Milstein Division of United States History, Local History & Genealogy, The New York Public Library, Astor, Lenox and Tilden Foundations

Page 244: 1880 cabinet card photographed by H. B. Lindsley

Page 247: Library of Congress, Prints & Photographs Division, NY, 31-NEYO, 11-1

The publishers wish to thank Tim Harris and Tara Key for their meticulous fact-checking and editing, and Douglas Matthews for his equally careful index.